For Loop, Hayley, Jimmy and Sunshine

Edited by Victoria Taylor

INTRODUCTION

With a couple of minutes to go, me and my Brother Shay gave each other 'the nod'. This non verbal communication meant that as soon as the final whistle went we were offskis. It was also conceding defeat, but there was always hope for one more chance. They say it's the hope that kills you but this is Manchester United and they never lost, they just ran out of time. The Third Official held up a board saying 3. Michael Jordan had his Last Dance, this was *'The Final Countdown'*.

When Teddy equalised it was an incredible feeling of relief, not just that we were still in the Champions League Final but because this whole adventure that we had dared to dream about wasn't going to end with a damp squib. We hugged wildly as our shins were battered on the seats in front of us, the bag I had held almost went flying into the tier above us and Shay was now wearing a baseball cap that he wasn't wearing before.

When we finally came up for air we had another corner. We all know what happened next but as I turned to my big Brother in disbelief, he wasn't there! I somehow knew to look down and he lay across the floor, having fainted when Solskjaer scored. I knelt to be at his level and for those few moments, despite the pandemonium going on around us, we felt like we were the only two people in The Nou Camp. Limbs were everywhere, flares were being set off and Big Pete was cartwheeling but we noticed none of that. Just a simple conversation as if we were back on Ascot Drive.

"Is that another goal?" He asked as he quickly came round.

"Yes, yes it is" I answered smiling.

"It can't be another goal?" he spluttered, tears and snot going everywhere.

"It is! It's 2-1!"

"Well get me up then you daft cunt!"

His power of recovery was remarkable and we partied like it was *1999* but how did we get here? How did we finally get to see The Promised Land of winning the European Cup? Well for that we have to go a very long way back to a cold night in F Stand and Widzew Łódź.

1. IF THE KIDS ARE UNITED

Whether or not I was going to be a United fan or not was never in question. I come from a long line of United supporting Taylors. They say that if you take a map of where you live and draw a line with a pencil and ruler to the nearest football ground then that should be your team. This was the case for me unless you include Flixton Football Club at Valley Road, although I have seen United play at Flixton. Fergie took a team there to mark the opening of the new floodlights on the Tuesday after the 5-1 massacre at Maine Road. Lee Sharpe, Mark Robins and Darren Ferguson were in the team although my personal highlight was after the game where people went on the pitch for a kick-about. I caught a volley on the full which flew over the bar and smashed into some poor sod serving in the burger van!

Anyway the story goes that my Great Grandad lived in the Bradford area of Manchester, not a million miles from where the Etihad is now. When the Reds moved from Bank Street (think where the Velodrome is) to Old Trafford it was a disaster. He got fed up of walking there and back so moved to Stretford to be closer. The family moved to Ireland after my Grandad fell in love but eventually returned to settle in South Manchester. This was and still is big United country and The Busby Babes used to play Golf at Davyhulme Golf Club every Monday. This was great for my Dad in getting their autographs and he also used to listen to the FA Cup Draw on the wireless before cycling to the course to tell them the draw.

I was the youngest of four, one Brother Shay and two Sisters, Clare and Marie and we were all reds of course. However my parents' marriage split up when I was 4 years old and in 1978 when I was six years old I went to my first United match. It was a 3-1 defeat to Bristol City and I have no recollection of it whatsoever. It's only because my Step Brother insisted that I did go that I know anything about it. We will move onto him later. Slowly I got a few games under my belt, under the moribund tutorship of Dave Sexton. I didn't really know that his football was boring because it was all that I knew but I did understand that we shouldn't be chanting

"What a load of rubbish!"

Then one night my Dad took me to my first European game against a team I had never heard of, Widzew Łódź of Poland. It was my first time in F Stand, tucked away next to the open section of the Stretford End, the dodgy little brother of the 'Cantilever' Stand with its sweeping stand length concourse. The teams entered and I was horrified, we were wearing BLACK SHORTS... at home! We never wore black shorts at home! I convinced myself that Assistant Manager/Physiotherapist Tommy Cavanagh had made a terrible mistake and he was going to have to be relieved of his services. You know when you are about to take off or land in a plane, you watch the air stewardesses to see if they look worried, well I was looking at the United players for that reassurance. It was only when he ran onto collect the players tracksuits and no one was giving him pelters that I realised things were ok.

United led from a Sammy Mac goal but the undoubted star of the show was future Juventus forward, Zbigniew Boniek. He was rapid and ran the bollocks off our Right Back Jimmy Nicholl. After he got fouled for the umpteenth time he rolled around... and rolled, and rolled, and rolled. The Polish Physio ran on and so did two other blokes in trench coats. This European football was full of surprises! Such was the extent of Boniek's acting that I thought the two extras were possibly priests administering The Last Rites or even Undertakers ready to declare the time of death. He rose Lazarus style though and from one of the free kicks he won, Krzysztof Surlit hit an absolute thundertwat of a free kick to send the coach load of Poles down from Crumpsall

Polish Club into rapture. It also proved to be the winning goal as two weeks later a goalless draw sent United out on Away Goals. The European Dream was over for another season and so was Dave Sexton. Despite 7 straight wins at the end of the season he was sacked in May and the search for a new manager began. Enter Big Fat Ron from Old Swan.

2. DA DOO RON RON

I didn't know much about Ron Atkinson to be fair but anything had to be better than Sexton so there was excitement at his arrival. His initial foray into the transfer market saw John Gidman arrive from Everton and Frank Stapleton from Arsenal. 'Frankie Lad' was especially welcome in our house as both my Sisters fancied him. One player he inherited was Gary Birtles. His tenure at Old Trafford had been a disastrous one and he still hadn't scored a league goal a year after Sexton signed him. The joke was that the first thing the American hostages said upon their return from Iran was

"Has Birtles scored yet?" Well eventually he did at home to Swansea and I was sat on the back row of K Stand. Being on the back row you could see into the private boxes and I was having a good nosey when I just turned around in time to see Birtles twat one in from 30 yards or so. Every year it seems to get further and further out! There were no cameras there that day so no one has ever seen the goal again and everyone has different memories of it! He managed to bag a few more that year but was sold back to Forest the following season.

The other arrivals both came from West Bromwich Albion. Local lad Remi Moses and in a British record transfer, Bryan Robson. Robbo famously signed on the pitch before a 5-0 win against Wolves. One of those 'I was there' games. Unfortunately I wasn't there. I had gone to Woodsend with Dave Merron to buy a single from the new record shop. We didn't have enough to buy one each so we bought a copy of 'Shut Up' by Madness on 7" and agreed to keep it for 6 months each. A bit like the Charity Shield (the traditional curtain raiser to the English Season). When I got home and heard Robson had signed on the pitch in his suit and then we won 5-0 well I naturally had visions of him powering through midfield in his suit. A look he later copied when he signed for Middlesbrough as Player/Manager, his photo shoot on the pitch consisted of him wearing a suit on his top half and a football kit on his bottom half.

Although I wasn't at that game I did go to his home debut against Spurs in the Milk Cup. We lost 1-0. There was another early exit in the FA Cup away at Watford so the season pretty much coasted to its finish as the team bonded together. The final bit of excitement came with the debut of Norman Whiteside. He was only 16 when he came on as sub versus Brighton and it was to be a short but spectacular career where the records seemed to chase him. Youngest player to play in the World Cup Finals, score in a League Cup Final and score in an FA Cup Final. He repeated his Wembley heroics with the winner in the 1985 FA Cup Final vs Everton and his Scouse Busting Don't give a shit attitude made him a fans favourite and he was definitely a favourite of mine.

Years later I was a Saturday Dad and that often used to mean a trip to The Wheatsheaf in Altrincham, where they showed the reds on the hooky foreign channels and had a big play area out the back. Whiteside was a regular there, keeping himself to himself with his favourite tipple being Red Wine and Diet Coke. As the visits became more frequent we found ourselves on nodding terms and one time, my Daughter and Whiteside's Son sat playing Top Trumps whilst I got to sit with the big man himself. He was impressed that I remembered his home debut vs Stoke (I was there) and his goal was one of the highlights of that season. The 'Thanks a Million' banner came out as always before the final game of the season but we wanted to see the Reds parading trophies not banners. We didn't have long to wait.

3. OH BROTHER!

My match day experience was starting to take shape. Either my Dad or my Brother Shay would drive and they would park in the Norweb Sub Station on Chester Road. The substation was like Platform 9 and 3/4. It's always been there, still is in fact but you only see it if you look hard enough. They both worked for Norweb so had a key to the padlock on the front and they got a great parking spot. A few years later we would upgrade to the Norweb Sports and Social Club on Talbot Road. Back to 1982 and we would split up into three groups. My Dad sat in the cantilever with his Brother, my Uncle Danny. He owned his own hairdressing salon in Chester (make of that what you will) and was one of the nicest blokes you will ever meet. We would all go there to get our hair cut and it would be a competition as to who would see 'Face Mountain' first on the M53. Speaking of hair, we were blessed with the Ginger gene. The balding with glasses and a Ginger/grey beard that I have now, was what my Dad was sporting in those days. As he got older he started to look like Harold Shipman and Malcolm Glazer. Hobson's choice really. He didn't think his lookalikes could get any worse until they pulled Saddam Hussein out of that hole.

Shay would be with his Girlfriend Denise. He seemed to have a ticket in every stand so you were never quite sure where he would be sat or stood. More often than not I was with my Step Brother Paul. My parents split up when I was 4 years old. Being the youngest of four I was protected from any potential fall out and didn't really have to do very much for myself. Two years later and Dad was back in a relationship and that's how my eventual future step brother came into my life. Right from the get go when he told me (spoiler alert) that Father Christmas wasn't real, he was a cunt. A bullying cunt at that. Physical, mental and even sexual he had a hold on me for years. Even now as a 50 year old Father of three, once I have finished watching a television programme I will put the sound on mute, just like I used to when I was a teenager, just in case he heard my telly from his bedroom and would come in to abuse me some more. Let's make one thing clear, at no point did he try and force himself upon me. However he did used to make me watch him masturbate to completion, so is that sexual abuse? He also devised a game called 'Naked Grange Hill' which consisted of us pretending we were at Grange Hill school, whilst naked of course. And he always got to be Tucker Jenkins, the twat!

Of course from the outside it looked like the two of us were having a great time at the game as I laughed at all his jokes and tried to keep the conversation going so he didn't get bored and punch me on the same spot until it turned purple. We would go to the shop on Railway Road to buy a plastic bottle of orange juice and then over the steps to the Stretford End of the stadium. It would be another couple of years before I actually stood on The Stretford End. The majority of games I went to I would be in E Stand or 'The Stretford End seats' as it was known. A lot of people probably don't realise that there were a few hundred seats at the back of The Stretford End. I say seats, it was actually long wooden benches with a metal arm rest between each seat and enough arse and leg room for a very skinny 12 year old. You had to be in the queue for about 1pm as they would often lock the doors about 1.30pm as the stand was full. You had to buy the match programme for the all important token which hopefully would be stuck upon a token sheet later in the season. The closer United got to Wembley, the greater the sales of Pritt Stick in the Manchester area. After reading the programme, you could put your programme under the seat knowing that nobody would steal it. They never did. In fact the only time I did have a programme stolen from under my seat was when my Dad took me in The Old Stand for an FA Cup tie with West Ham in 1983. This missing token would cause problems further down the line.

Like this Dalliance in D Stand, there would be occasional games in different parts of the stadium but my formative years were done at the most popular end of the stadium. Not in the heaving, swaying hotbed of masculinity, be it left side or right side or if you shouted for Celtic or Rangers, you were a 'Stretford Ender', well just above it anyway.

4. SHE WORE A SCARLET RIBBON

The new season began with three new signings. Two Peters and an Arnold. Bodak and Beardsley didn't play 90 minutes between them but Muhren was a success coming in from Ipswich Town. This season also saw the return of European Football as we had qualified for the UEFA Cup and first up was a far more glamorous tie than Widzew Łódź with the visit of Valencia from Spain, complete with World Cup winner Mario Kempes. This was also a memorable night as it was my mate Darren's first United match. Darren was my best mate growing up, he lived three doors down and we were very fortunate to have a big field outside our house. It also wasn't visible from the main road so we didn't get passing trade as it were. A form of headers and volleys was our game of choice which we called 'Records' as you kept trying to beat the Record for the most goals scored past one keeper. That summer was the Spain 82 World Cup and we all decided to be an international player to add spice to the game. I was Diego Maradona, Darren was Michel Platini and Paul Collinge was inexplicably Paul Mariner. One advantage of doing volleys all day is that although I wasn't a particularly good footballer, I was bloody brilliant at volleys. Even better still, I could do overhead kicks. Starting with side on volleys like Zico or Berbatov into full blown Mark Hughes like overhead kicks. Indeed a dream came true when I scored one in a game when I was about 30 years old. A proper 'Rooney vs City' effort, the only problem was I didn't actually see it hit the net and there is still a tiny part of me that thinks it was all a massive wind up when they celebrated and it actually landed somewhere on Barton Bridge. Nah, surely not? Maybe that's why the JJB Soccer Dome won't put a blue plaque up on the sight of the goal despite my constant petitioning.

Darren had a strange knack of looking like every Black footballer, be it Des Walker, Fat Ronaldo or Oman-Bayik. He was very much Remi Moses at this time. Anyway he had finally been allowed to come to a game with us and sat in the E Stand with me. It was a very old fashioned bruising encounter with Valencia kicking United off the park, rolling around everywhere and generally getting up to Johnny Foreigner shenanigans. Daz learnt a new song that night...

"YOU DIRTY SPANISH BASTARDS!!" we sang over and over as one dreadful foul followed another. After a disappointing 0-0 draw we ruminated on events in the car home and it turned out that Shay had been sitting just a few rows behind us and had heard us singing our new song all night. He also accused me of sticking V Signs up at the Spanish keeper and he knew it was me because I had dirty fingernails! A couple of weeks later we were huddled around our Music Centre (this was 1982) listening to Tom Tyrrell's commentary from The Mestella. I used to love those commentary games on Piccadilly Radio. Although the commentary style wasn't a patch on Peter Jones or Mike Ingham over on Radio 2, you always felt that Tom was down in the trenches as he would often be sat in amongst the away supporters doing his commentary. Indeed one time at Stamford Bridge in 1991 he did get thrown out when some cockney tool grabbed his phone and shouted

"You dirty northern slaaaags!"down the line. I missed this though as I was actually there that day in the United end. For this commentary though I was behind the sofa as we tried to defend a lead given to us by the magnificent Robson. You could tell from the crackly radio commentary that things weren't going United's way on or off the pitch as we were on the receiving end of some dodgy refereeing decisions and dodgy Spanish police attacking our fans. The quest for European glory fell at the first hurdle as we capitulated to a 2-1 defeat.

Things were looking better in the other two competitions though as we found ourselves in the semi final of both the Milk

Cup and the FA Cup and we were to play Arsenal both times. We battered them at Highbury 4-2 and were supremely confident going into the Second Leg for my first semi final. A regulation 2-1 win saw us qualify for a Wembley final for the first time since 1979 although that wasn't the most memorable event that night. Over in Coronation Street, Deirdre Barlow and Mike Baldwin were having an affair and it looked like Ken was going to confront them. There was no Sky Plus though, we didn't even have a Video Recorder yet so if something was on when you were out then you missed it! Half Time at OT and the big news is flashed on the scoreboard...

"KEN AND DEIRDRE ARE REUNITED!" cue massive cheers from the Northerners and chants of '

"There's only one Mike Baldwin' from the cockneys."

In the FA Cup Semi Final, I was listening to the radio again as the rest of the family went to Villa Park for the game. Once again it was Robson and Whiteside who were the inspiration and we were in the FA Cup Final against unfancied Brighton and Hove Albion. Now remember that programme I had pinched from under my seat in the old stand? Come on it was only in the last chapter! Anyway that meant I was a token down on everyone else and ruled me out of going to either final and first up was the old enemy Liverpool in the Milk Cup Final. This was to be the last final that wasn't shown Live on the telly so I was listening on the radio again and for the second half of the season there was a different commentator on Piccadilly... Richard Keys. That's right, old hairy hands used to commentate on United games and his ballooning after Stapleton's injury time winner vs Everton in the Quarter Final was superb. Sadly the gods were against us again or at least George Courtney was, and we lost 2-1. My Dad and Shay were very keen to watch the highlights the next day if only to see Norman Whiteside's goal which they said was fantastic.

"This is it" they said as Gordon McQueen launched one forward when the house was plunged into silence as the Electric had run out! 'Shit! Who's got 50p!' By the time we found one the Liverpool players were trudging back to the halfway line after the goal!

Come the Cup Final and it was just me and my Sister again as the others went to Wembley. I was also very ill around that time as I was suffering from Hepatitis. I had been off school for a couple of weeks and I even got a visit from my school pals the night before the replay and they had all made me get well cards with their predictions on them. They weren't allowed in though as my Dad was watching the European Cup Final! There wasn't much live football on telly in those days so you watched everything. He decided against going to the replay and I was very happy to be with him to celebrate my first trophy as a United fan. Now don't forget I was still very poorly and very infectious but we had just won the Cup and my Dad wanted to celebrate so he dragged me and Marie down to the Railway Tavern and left us outside with the ubiquitous bottle of coke and a packet of crisps! First trophy in the cabinet, what would the Cup Winners Cup have in store for us?

5. GAGARIN

Three months after United's Wembley victory over Brighton, the Reds returned to the Twin Towers for the 4th time that season against Liverpool in the Charity Shield (the traditional curtain raiser to the English season). Sorry but you can't say one without the other. Let's try. The Charity Shield (the traditional curtain raiser to the English season). See! For me however, it was my first time at the National Stadium and I was very excited. The whole day was a new experience for me. Even the journey into Town to catch the train was new to me. I can't recall ever being in Piccadilly before and I remember seeing a massive JVC sign and thinking it was like being in Times Square.

Unlike future London awayers which would begin by taking over a boozer somewhere, we went straight into the ground and my first view of the sacred ground of Wembley and what a shithole! I couldn't wait to get into my seat though to 'take in the atmosphere'. It was about 90 minutes before kick off and nothing to see but I was lapping it up. The rest stayed in 'The Long Bar'. This was the first match since Bob Paisley had stepped down as Liverpool manager and before the game he rode around the pitch in a Popemobile with Sir Matt Busby. An attempt to bring some peace and harmony after a load of mither at the Milk Cup Final between the two six months before.

Graham was our only new signing. Something of a journeyman winger bought from Leeds and he had a great debut. However it was Bryan Robson who followed up his brace on his last club appearance here with another two goal salvo in a 2-0 win. This of course meant I had my first experience of 'ballooning' when we scored. Celebrating a goal away from home is a very different experience to at Old Trafford and many a time I've enjoyed a good 'limbs everywhere' celebration.

I wouldn't return to Wembley for another 7 years, at least not to support United. I did go to the Football League Centenary game in 1987, a brilliant birthday present from Shay. Some of the best players in the world were playing including Diego Maradona and Michel Platini (Paul Mariner never made the cut) but it would be our very own World Class Bryan Robson who scored another 2 goals for the Football League XI (are you beginning to spot the pattern? There will be another Robbo brace before the book has ended) and even better than that, The Wheatsheaf's very own Norman Whiteside added the third in a 3-0 win. My overriding memory however was something that happened in the Wembley toilets after the game. There was a long urinal which ran the length of the wall and everyone was pissing into it except one bloke. I was heading for the exit when I made eye contact with a Scandinavian looking bloke who was facing away from the piss stones and squatting. As I got closer I discovered to my horror that he was having a shit. A great big Mr Whippy one at that. To this day I will never know if he couldn't wait for the one sit down toilet that people were queuing for or whether he was indeed European and this was the normal thing to do? I've seen those holes in the floor in Parisian toilets!

The season got off to a good start including beating Liverpool again. The Cup Winners Cup campaign got off to an inconspicuous start. A last minute Ray Wilkins penalty salvaged a draw and kept our unbeaten home record in Europe intact. As a massive Half Man Half Biscuit fan I was unaware of the irony of seeing Dukla Prague in their Away Kit. The reds got a 2-2 draw in the second leg sneaking through on away goals. Things were a lot easier in the Second Round vs Spartak Varna who played in the wonderfully named Yuri Gagarin Stadium. As a massive Public Service Broadcasting fan I was unaware of the irony of the stadium name. Things would be a lot more difficult in the Quarter Final... bring on Diego and Barcelona.

6. LOCK UP YOUR MOUNTAIN BIKES

Big Ron had a problem. Misfiring forwards. Frank Stapleton was never going to break goal scoring records and Norman Whiteside was having the footballing equivalent of a 'difficult second album'. Atkinson clearly didn't rate Beardsley and although he had given Mark Hughes his debut vs Oxford United that only came about because Arthur Graham had the shits. He didn't trust Hughes yet. So he looked to an unlikely source for goals with a loan move for Garth Crooks. This did have the desired effect albeit indirectly as on Crooks home debut, Stapleton scored a Hat Trick versus Watford. This was the first Hat Trick I had ever seen in the flesh... What was yours?

The future Football Focus Fuckstick, Crooks, only weighed in with two goals and was sent packing back to Spurs. Those two goals did help me out once though. 1999-2000 season and ITV's pay TV channel On Digital got the rights to the Champions League games that weren't on the main channel with Clive. No one had On Digital. Hell, not even the pubs had On Digital. One of these games was United's trip to Marseille for a group game. One of my Dad's friends, Francis, had managed to get hold of Two tickets for a screening of the game at the Ford Showroom on the end of Sir Matt Busby Way and asked if I would like to go. When we got there we were amused to find that there was a panel there to review the game and do the old Half Time chat. The event was hosted by Ray Stubbs and the panel was Mark Lawrenson and Garth *'Two Goals'* Crooks. So far so good. The only problem was that the signal wasn't very good. You know when you watch the game online and it freezes and stutters, well this is how this game was. After a couple of interruptions in the first half, the Second Half was like watching Norman Collier play and soon enough the signal was lost completely. Lawro and

Crooksy did the best they could to fill in but the natives were getting restless. Then somebody had a brain wave. We were sat in a car showroom and what does every car have? A radio! Just tune them all into Five Live and turn them to full volume and Bob's yer uncle, Fannys yer aunt and Dick's yer Mum's best friend. So the staff turned all the radios up and yes, we could just hear a commentary...

"And that's Arsenal 2 Barcelona 4 here at Wembley."
Five Live had a different game on!

Anyhow there was a quiz at Half Time and the question was 'how many goals did Garth Crooks score in his career and how many for United?' Well I think we can all work out that I got the second part of the question right and was quietly confident with my guess of a nice round 150 career goals. Sure enough I was closest and victorious and my prize was 2 tickets for a future Champions League game as guests of Ford. Fuck me I'm gonna be sat in the posh seats here and I suppose it makes sense to return the favour and invite Francis. The future Champions League game turned out to be a dead rubber against Sturm Graz and I was sat in The Family Stand! And to make matters worse it was one of those games where United had given out free tickets to all the local schools so we had ear screeching chants, attempted Mexican Waves and the 10 second countdown on the scoreboard. '10! 9! 8! 7! 6! 5! 4! 3! 2! 1! Screeeeam!' and then massive disappointment as Alan Keegan announces a minimum of three minutes of injury time. Half Man Half Biscuit once sang that

"*With the possible exception of being Garth Crooks there is surely nothing worse than washing sieves*". Thanks Garth, thanks for nothing, apart from 2 goals.

7. 2,3,GO

Diego Armando Maradona. There is always something special about someone who is afforded the middle name treatment. Elvis Aaron Presley, John Fitzgerald Kennedy, Stanley Victor Collymore... well 2 out of 3 ain't bad(Michael Lee Aday). Everybody knew Maradona was a genius but to be honest we based it on very little. There was no coverage of Spanish Football, never mind Argentinian Football over here and he had a poor 1982 World Cup culminating in a sending off vs Brazil. He played against England as a kid in 1980 but we weren't blessed with many sightings in the flesh. In fact I only ever think he played in this country 5 times and I was at 2 of them. England vs Argentina 1980 as mentioned, United vs Barcelona 1984 going to be mentioned. Ossie Ardiles Testimonial 1986 he turned out for Spurs, Football League vs Rest of World (ROW) 1987 remember the guy having a shit in the urinal? Soccer Aid 2006 Old Trafford again as Maradona successfully scored a penalty past Jamie Theakston.

Even so we were very excited when the draw was made and I was going to see the man I chose to be playing headers and volleys back home at Ascot Drive. Once again we sat and listened to the radio for the first leg at Camp Nou. The reds started well but Aberdonian Cart Horse Graeme Hogg scored an unfortunate own goal. Still we made some good chances and Robbo for once was culpable. We were just about to settle for a 1-0 defeat, when Juan Carlos Rojo scored an absolute worldie and it looked like the Second Leg would be an anti climax.

Unlike the previous season I had a full token sheet so managed to get a ticket for the home leg although this did include the now lost art of queuing all night outside Old Trafford waiting for the ticket office to open. Another bonus was that Shay had managed to get tickets for the Europa Suite. He sold tickets for the Manchester United Development Association (raffle tickets I guess) and one of the perks was getting tickets for the Europa Suite. This was a lounge in the Old Stand with a bar and a telly. Sometimes the players would even pop in there after a game which was very exciting for this 11 year old. I still call it The Old Stand. None of this South Stand, Main Stand or Sir Bobby Charlton Stand bollocks. My mate John's Dad called the chippy on Moss Road in Stretford 'Beardwoods' years after it had changed hands.

As luck would have it we were in the Old Stand for the game, on the very back row of B Stand (probably where the TV Box is now that the pundits sit in when games are on telly). We got there very early and I was amazed at how busy it already was. I saw Sir Matt Busby on the forecourt and got him to sign my programme. I was secretly even more excited with the second autograph I got, Alex Higgins!

Come kick off and the noise was absolutely deafening. The Reds had gone top of the league on the Saturday before with a Robson inspired thumping of Arsenal and confidence was high. Such was Robbo's influence on the team that the fans produced a ROBSON MUST STAY petition before the game which we signed at the bottom of the Railway Bridge steps. The Italians were circling with both AC Milan and Juventus interested. With hardly any Barcelona fans present, it was a red hot atmosphere and it was to get even hotter when Robson gave United the lead, stooping to conquer at the back post from a Hogg flick on. 1-0 was good at Half Time but within 5 minutes of the restart, all hell broke loose.

First Barca keeper Urutti kicked weakly and then spilled an even weaker shot from Wilkins for a rampant Robson to make it 2-0. Unbelievably we had pulled the tie level.

"Robson suddenly finds himself on a European Hat Trick" said commentator Martin Tyler as Captain Marvel swept it out to Arthur Albiston who sent in a left foot cross...

"Whiteside... STAPLETON! 2 GOALS IN 2 MINUTES! IT'S A GLORIOUS NIGHT FOR MANCHESTER UNITED!" The roof nearly came off Old Trafford. Absolute bedlam.

"Here we go! Here we go! Here we go!" This was the ubiquitous chant of the Stretford End but it sounded fucking incredible! Then something even more incredible... something my Dad said he hadn't seen for years, they were singing in the seats! They were actually singing in the seats! Not just the Stretford End seats where I was usually to be found, but all around the ground including the Cantilever Stand, home to the cigar munching season ticket holders.

This was footballing nirvana, an atmosphere and result we would talk about for years to come, maybe people may even write books about it. There was only one problem there were still 35 minutes to go! As Big Ron acknowledged in his interview with Elton Welsby after the game, we had scored far too early and there was another cigar munching gentleman who was plotting against us... the Barca manager Cesar Luis Menotti. The Blaugrana may have been wearing yellow but they were getting more and more into the game, giving hope to the few travelling Culers. Maradona was being marked out of the game by Aberdeen War Horse and forgiven legend Graeme Hogg but it was the German Bernd Schuster who was causing the problems as his influence on the game grew. The Catalans started to pepper Gary Bailey's goal with shots, substitute Mark Hughes was lucky not to give away a penalty whilst Maradona dived more in hope than expectation to try and win one.

The last 10 minutes felt like about 3 days but when the referee blew the final whistle, pandemonium ensued. United had pulled off one of the greatest victories in their history and this merited a pitch invasion. Thousands of reds with perry boy haircuts and casual Lyle & Scott leisurewear poured onto the pitch and lifted Captain Marvel shoulder high. As for us, well we definitely wanted to invade the pitch but we were on the back row of B Stand remember, so I had to settle for being lifted onto the shoulders of some random bloke so I could see what was going on and cheer into the Mancunian night. I certainly didn't ask for this mini Glastonbury experience and maybe he held me by my thighs for a little too long but this was the 80's after all.I could also see from my new lofty point that I couldn't see any of my family who I was at the match with. Shit. Top red that I am, I burst into tears straight away. Then I remembered we were going to the Europa Suite but had no idea how to get there. I told my pervy friend and he didn't just know how to get there but led me through the Directors Box to the door. I wonder if he remembers this encounter from his cell as much as I do? Anyway I waited for a while but still no sign of my Dad, Shay, Denise or Paul. After 10 minutes or so I managed to persuade the Hector on the door that I was just going to have a look inside when sure enough, they were all sitting around a table with pints galore! They hadn't even noticed I wasn't there! I felt like Kevin from Home Alone!

Even better of course was that we could stay in The Europa Suite and wait for the highlights on the big screen. No Live European matches in those days of course so Sportsnight or in this case Midweek Sports Special was essential viewing. This is part of the magic of this game, there was no countrywide shared experience of Live coverage or even banal banter back in the BT Sport Studio, this was a real "I was there!" moment and I was. Without doubt this was the greatest night I ever saw at Old Trafford.

One last footnote is that before our game came on, there was a report on how Liverpool were getting on against Benfica in a game that hadn't finished yet. They were cruising through to the semis but the name of the young Radio City presenter pictured holding a phone was Clive Tyldsley. We will be hearing from him again.

8. TORINO

After the excitement of the Quarter Final vs Barcelona, you would think that the semi final would be even more exciting. We were drawn against another powerhouse in Juventus, with the first leg to be played at Home. As we discovered in the last game, a result is never certain after the first leg meaning they were often cagey affairs.

First things first was getting the tickets. With little time between the Quarter Final and the semis, the tickets went on sale during the week. Obviously my Dad couldn't bunk off work to queue for tickets but he had no problems with sending my Sister Marie, who was a month or so short of taking her O Levels, to queue for them before going into School at Cardinal Vaughan.

By all rights Vecchia Signora should have battered us. They had the likes of Platini, Boniek, Tardelli and Rossi up against our injury-hit midfield of Moses, McGrath, Gidman and Graham. Paolo Rossi scored for Juve via a deflection off Aberdonian Cart Horse again Graeme Hogg. Then John Gidman went off with a dislocated perm (in his first match for months) and was replaced by Alan Davies (in his first match for months). It was actually his first match for United since the FA Cup Final Replay 11 months before. He played one game for Wales vs Brazil and then suffered a serious injury. So he played FA Cup Final, Brazil vs Juventus. Not just that, he scored the equaliser. This was to be the pinnacle of his career though and sadly he committed suicide in 1992.

I was in the Cantilever Stand for this game and even though the crowd was slightly larger than the Barcelona game, the vociferous atmosphere just wasn't there. And so to the Second Leg in Turin and as you can probably guess The Taylor Family was crowded around the radio. The Final was to be held in Basel,

Switzerland and my Dad and Shay had made their plans to go. A minibus was mentioned and time off tentatively booked. They needn't have bothered. Despite a battling 1-1 score line bringing parity to the tie (and a heroic performance from Gary Bailey) Paolo Rossi broke United hearts with a last minute winner. Absolute heartbreak. This is the only time in my life that I saw my Big Brother cry. I mean probably sob. The dream had gone and so had the league title. Some new blood was needed.

9. THE HEADMASTER RITUAL

During the previous season I made a big move of my own. I passed my 11+ exam despite Hepatitis flooring me for a few weeks and I was put forward for the St Bede's College Entrance Examination and much to my surprise, I passed and was offered a place. I had expected to go to St Paul's in Urmston like the rest of my class did. I loved it at my Primary School, St Monica's in Flixton where I was a popular 'joker in the pack' and it brought me a sweet escape from 'Naked Grange Hill' and beatings off my Step Brother at weekend. Obviously I had excelled academically there but it was also a right good laugh. Back in the day and before my balls had dropped I had a fantastic singing voice. Proper choirboy stuff and I got to sing solo in Manchester Cathedral in front of the Bishop of Manchester. It was good practice for singing in front of Bishop Blaize in later life.

Back at school I got offered the role of The Tinman in our school production of *'The Wizard of Oz'* and I was comfortably the best singer there. Come opening night and I glanced out from backstage to see all the Mums, Dads and Mummy's new friend's wafting paper fans in front of their faces as it had probably been the hottest day of the year. The Tinman makes his entrance shortly before the interval and my song *'If I Only Had a Heart'* is a barnstorming success and I even had to sing it twice as the crowd demanded an encore. We come off for the interval and I start feeling unwell. I'm wearing a fucking tinfoil outfit and I'm basically cooking like a Christmas Turkey on the stage! I'm now throwing up in the toilet and panicking that they may have to cancel the second half of the show. This of course never crossed the mind of Sister Cecilia our battle axe Headmistress, she was a Nun from the Sisters of Notre Dame order although not as bad as Sister Fucking Mary. They simply removed the tinfoil from my outfit and made an announcement that the Tin Man would be appearing in the second half without his Tin (to an empathetic ahhh from the audience).

I felt a bit better and had a hand held fan so all was good. Oh look, there's Christina Bridge (she was to be my first kiss) in a tank top and oh look, I can just glimpse a bra strap and then it happened... I get a fucking prepubescent Hard On whilst wearing an all in one felt number. Thank fuck for my Tinman's Axe to protect my modesty! Also thank god this was in the days before iPhones and the like otherwise I probably would have ended up on Lad Bible by now with the headline '*The Wizard of Rods*'. Thankfully I had a new outfit for the second night that was tantamount to a sleeping bag but at least I could get a stiffy in peace.

St Bede's was a whole different ball game. Originally built in the salubrious area of Whalley Range, and built in the Italian Renaissance Style, Bede's was one of the Top Independent Catholic Schools in the Country but still very regimented. Former pupil and Folk Singer Mike Harding described it as 'a Catholic Tom Brown's School Days with frankincense, the Latin Mass and buggery'.I had absolutely no idea where Whalley Range was other than our Shay saying it was near City's Ground in Moss Side. Of course it wasn't a salubrious area anymore and the riots had only been two years previous. It wasn't a safe place for an 11 year old to walk around carrying a briefcase but that's exactly what happened. They didn't do cross country as such at Bede's but you ran around Alexandra Park which was opposite the school. Unfortunately the locals used to like to 'pick off' any stray runner and sometimes you would get credit for breaking your PB when in fact you were running full pelt to escape getting mugged.

A plan was made for me to catch my first bus (the 257 from Towns Gate to Trafford Bar) and then get the 53 (affectionately known as 'The African Queen because' it went fucking everywhere) to Brooks Bar and then a 10 minute walk. I still can't get my head around the fact that I was allowed to do this every day at that age but what choice did I have? Coming from Trafford, I didn't have to pay for my tuition unlike most of the rest of my class. It wasn't just my classmates who let me know this but the staff too. I got called a Trafford Tramp on my first day by my form tutor, Father Paxton.

"Jimmy and daddy." Sorry my young son, Jimmy just came and typed that. I'd best leave it in.

At St Monica's I was Captain of the school football team. I wasn't first choice but Kieron Hughes lost the captaincy in a club vs. country type battle. Well actually he was playing for Flixton Juniors and didn't want to get injured playing for the school team. I was made Captain on account of doing a slide tackle in a game. It also meant I was now playing centre half. Our star player was undoubtedly Peter Thorne. He was in the year below us at school and comfortably the best player I had ever seen. He went on to play for Blackburn Rovers, including playing against United at Wembley in the Charity Shield (the traditional curtain raise to the English season) and then carved out a successful career at both Stoke City and Cardiff City.

I didn't fare as well at Bede's, although it did get me out of the house. I was the only person who didn't enjoy the holidays as it meant I was alone at home with Paul. I would get up early and sneak out of the house and walk for miles usually to my cousin Debbie's in Flixton. Solvitur ambulando 'it is solved by walking'. Someone at school also told me that Morrissey lived at 384 Kings Road in Stretford and the 15 bus went right there from outside our house. So a few times I went and stood outside his house with other Smiths fans (he was never in) before going to the chippy at The Quadrant for my dinner.

My greatest achievement at School was getting suspended for having blonde streaks in my hair. I had gone to my Uncle Danny's shop in Chester and asked the girls to make me look like Barney

Sumner from New Order. The headmaster, Mr Byrne, took one look and sent me home. Originally he said 'until it grows out' which would have meant more time at home but I got called back after a couple of days. At Football I only made the B Team so there were no real opportunities for me to do any volleys or overhead kicks. It wasn't the only thing I was overlooked for. Being a Boarding School for some, there was always a running joke that the priests were buggering the borders at night. Then it didn't really come as a shock to find Father Green got a 10 stretch at Strangeways. He never looked at me once! I had Barney Sumner streaks in my hair! We could have played Naked Songs of Praise!

One of my school reports said 'If he put as much effort into his schoolwork as he did into Manchester United then he would be at the top of the class instead of the bottom'. Never a truer word has been said.

10. THE QUEEN OF DENMARK

Big Ron spent big in the summer. Gordon Strachan came in from Aberdeen and Alan Brazil from Tottenham Hotspur. Big Ron's third summer signing however became my new favourite player: Jesper Olsen. Ever since he tore England apart playing for Denmark or took the famous 1-2 penalty with Johan Cruyff, I had wanted Olsen to sign for United. He wore his shirt outside his shorts like George Best, he played on the wing like George Best, he shagged a model like George Best, but that's where the comparison probably ended. When he arrived at United I instantly pretended I was him. I became Olsen on the field opposite my house playing 'records' and in my mind I would put myself in his place, doing false interviews after the game etc. and creating a whole new back story to explain why Philip Taylor had signed from Ajax and played for Denmark. I didn't always use my real name in my fantasies though. I used to pretend I was a goalkeeper called Steve Somersault and would write stories about his escapades (maybe that can be the follow up title). I would practice saves by throwing a box of Swan Vestas matches across my bed and then diving full length to catch them.

Olsen started well with early goals vs Chelsea and Newcastle but soon found the pace and general shithousery of the English First Division a bit too much. Strachan, however (as featured in the magnificent '*Strachan*' by The Hitchers) made a great start and was vying for top goal scorer alongside Mark Hughes. Brazil (as featured in the magnificent '*A Lilac Harry Quinn*' by Half Man Half Biscuit) was shit. He did bag his first Home goal in a 5-1 rout vs West Ham and the following week was Spurs at Home. This game always guaranteed a decent turn out and I rocked up at the E Stand turnstile to be greeted with huge queues. It didn't take long for the doors to shut meaning I was going to have to stand on The Stretford End! I entered onto the holy ground for the first time, towards the open section without the roof and I only had one question... where was I supposed to put my programme? With no seat to put it under I spent the whole game clinging onto it as if my life depended on it.

For once it wasn't Liverpool who were setting the pace but Everton. By the time they arrived at OT in March they were well out of sight. And what of our Three Musketeers who arrived with great fanfare. Olsen had disappointed but easily had his best United game yet. He scored his first goal for 6 months and was brought down for an early penalty. Strachan who had been prolific from the spot early on had missed a few and possibly saved his worst penalty for this game. A scuffed effort that was never going to trouble Southall. Alan Brazil made his first start for 2 months and had his sliding doors moment. Having assisted Olsen on the first, the Dane returned the favour putting him through. The ball did sit up though and Brazil contorted his body to hit a spectacular volley. The ball hit the underside of the bar and rebounded to safety. An inch lower and Brazil would have scored the winner and his whole United career could have been different. The game finished 1-1 and Everton would go on to be worthy champions.

Big Ron did love a cup run though and a Norman Whiteside Hat Trick in the Quarter Final vs West Ham saw us face Liverpool in the semi finals. United were very unlucky in the first game with the scousers equalising with a last minute offside goal. The replay at Maine Road would go down in United folklore with Robson and Hughes in true Scouse-busting form. Before going to school I saw Shay had left his programme on the table so I took it into school and cockily told everyone that I had been to the game. I regaled them with tales of moody encounters with Scousers on Great Western Road when I was actually listening at home on the radio. Of course I then told everyone I was going to the Cup Final too. The big day arrived and Big Norm kept up his

Wembley heroics to stop Everton adding to their Cup Winners Cup and winning a third trophy (NOT the Treble, there is only one Treble).

Now anyone who lives in the UDF (Urmston, Davyhulme and Flixton) will know that Woodsend Fair was always held on Cup Final Day. The Fair was the biggest event of the year and hanging round the Waltzers and 'keeping dog' looking out for the infamous Irlam Mob who never turned up (btw my predictive text changed Irlam Mob to Islam Mob. Good job I spotted that!). At full time we spilled out onto the field to try and recreate Whiteside's winner. My Dad and Shay were of course at Wembley so I could actually go on the Saturday Night to the Fair with the rest of my mates. One problem. Even though there were only a handful of kids at St Bede's who might have been at the fair, I couldn't risk running into someone when I was supposed to be at Wembley. Hung by my own bullshit petard!

The season had ended with a series of disasters. A 15 year old Leeds United fan was killed at St Andrews, Birmingham by a wall collapsing. This was overshadowed though by the Bradford City fire in which 56 people lost their lives. Finally there was Heysel. 39 Juventus fans killed trying to escape rampaging Liverpool fans. Yes the game should not have been played at such an unsafe stadium but it was undoubtedly Liverpool's fault. English Clubs were banned from Europe meaning the excellent Everton team were denied a crack at the European Cup and no Cup Winners Cup for United.

In May 1985 I also had a disaster of my own. We moved out of Ascot Drive and onto Stretford Road in Urmston. Two families together in a huge 3 storey house but nowhere for me to hide as I was put on the top floor with Paul. Having my own bedroom was great but I wished I was back in Flixton. Dark days were ahead.

11.   I WANT YOU

'No one ever said it was gonna be easy' sang The Inspiral Carpets with Mark E Smith on this chapter's titular song and merging the two houses of Ascot Drive and Tanhouse Road certainly wasn't. My Dad and Pat, my Sister Marie and Step Sister Jackie all had bedrooms on the first floor whilst myself and Paul had bedrooms upstairs. Shay and Denise stayed at Ascot Drive and I lived for the weekends when I got to go and stay there or Rossett Drive, the house they moved to in Davyhulme. Poor Denise must have had the patience of a saint putting up with me coming round every weekend. I didn't contribute to any of the cooking or cleaning because I knew no different. Any Live football match or the Mike Tyson title fights I would watch at Shay's. I would have gone round and watched the paint dry as long as I was away from Paul.Of course I didn't realise what I was doing back then but looking back it does make me cringe a bit and I do feel sorry for Denise.

I did love having my own room at home (which included a 6' Snooker Table I had got the Christmas before) but I hated its location right next to Paul's room. He would go out with his mates, get bladdered or high on 'Draw' and then come and take it all out on me. Not just was he a bully but a philosophical narcissistic one at that. He would spend hours asking me whether people liked him, whether he was ugly (he looked like a young Albert Steptoe) , cared about him or who he would win in a fight against. I don't know whether his constant weed habit lead to harder drugs but I know it lead him to a life of crime. In 1987 he tried robbing the Launderette directly opposite our house. He got to spend a few months at Thorn Cross detention centre in Warrington which was fine by me. I went to visit him a couple of times and we actually got on great. However the countdown was on and he eventually got his release date. June 9th 1988, my 16th Birthday. Many Happy Fucking Returns!

The Reds had got off to a blistering start winning the first ten games in a row. I was a regular in E Stand for all these home games and even saw Peter Shilton save a penalty! However as soon as I got to watch a few games in F Stand with Shay, they went off the boil. Michael Le Vell (Kevin Webster) was in F Stand also and I discovered when buying a programme that I was taller than him. I was 14 years old. Things went from bad to worse as word of Mark Hughes transfer to Barcelona got out and he was never the same player for the last few months. Big Ron being Big Ron decided to blow all of the Hughes money on Terry Gibson, Peter Davenport and John Sivebaek. Talk about panic buys. Having been 12 points clear in October they managed to finish a one horse race in Fourth place. Just for good measure, Liverpool completed the League and Cup double, the notion of which United achieving was just fanciful. Things got no better the following season and having heard rumours of Atkinson's sacking whilst at school, I rang Clubcall with my dinner money to hear the news confirmed. Enter Alexander Chapman Ferguson. Football, bloody hell.

12.   WE ARE FAMILY

Fergie's arrival also coincided with my first ever League Match Ticket Book (LMTB) of my own. Shay took one for the team and agreed to sit with me for two years in the Family Stand. It's also known as L Stand and it's where the Away Supporters sit now. We were two rows from the back but that didn't bother me. Having my own LMTB was a dream come true. They were one step down from a Season Ticket. Unlike today when there are about 50,000 Season Ticket Holders, in those days there were only about 5,000 and they were non transferable so if the Ticket Holder died then it was passed on in the family. My Grandad died in 1980 but my Dad had the Season Ticket right through until the amnesty when they built The North Stand in 1995. To put it another way, the majority of the Cantilever Stand was already dead.

Being The Family Stand then there were kids activities on. They promised celebrities and one week we got Roy Walker from Catchphrase, but generally it was squad players not selected so we pretty much ended up on nodding terms with Billy Garton. Oh I tell a lie, there was a local celebrity who was there every week handing out stickers and shit. It was Welephant the Fire Safety Elephant. Every. Fucking. Week.

So it was with much excitement and a roll full of Greater Manchester Fire Service stickers that I took my seat for the first home game vs West Ham. The Hammers scored after 30 seconds. 30 seconds! I've had some 30 second disappointments in my time but this one was a dagger to the heart and it didn't get much better. We did of course have the excitement of the new manager starting in November and John Sivebaek twatted home a free kick in his first game. After that we became a team capable of beating the best but inconsistent. We ended Arsenal's long unbeaten run with a Norman Whiteside inspired victory and a last minute Terry Gibson goal. Big Norm didn't score but kicked fuck out of them. We also put a massive dent in Liverpool's title chances with a last minute Peter Davenport goal. Who said they were desperate shit signings?

Brian McClair arrived the following season and he became the first United player to score 20 league goals since George Best. There were some good wins that season and we finished second but we were light years behind champions Liverpool. Our final game was an uneventful 2-1 win vs Wimbledon. Every week for 2 years when leaving we passed a lift and wondered where it went. Fuck it said Shay and we got in the lift and pressed UP. Where in the Theatre of Dreams would we end up? We ended up looking out of a window over the Munich clock and looking out over the forecourt. The crowd was sparse. There was no chance of mither as the Wimbledon fans had already left in their minibus. I had reached 16 and could no longer get a cheap LMTB in the Family Stand so it was back to The Stretford End for the next season, but winning the league still seemed light years away.

13.   4AD3DCD

The return of The Prodigal Son Leslie Mark Hughes from Barcelona cannot detract from what a pants season 88/89 was. There were sparks of excitement from Fergie's Fledglings, namely Messrs Sharpe, Martin, Robins, Beardsmore, Gill, Graham and The Cambridge Ronaldo, Guiliano Maiorana. There was an FA Cup Run culminating with a controversial home defeat to Nottingham Forest. Unfortunately this cup run tied in with the embarrassing national fad of Inflatables at Football matches. Forest's tricky trees, Grimsby's haddocks, United's tridents and city's Fucking Bananas. Cringe.

Once knocked out of the cup the season just ebbed away. There were 55,000 at the Quarter Final vs Forest and only 36,000 for the next Home game vs Luton. Shay and I were there in The Stretford End and sometimes people used to pay to go in The Stretford Paddock (which was slightly cheaper and had smaller queues) and then jump over into its more illustrious neighbour. That's what happened against Luton, just as Shay was biting into his Hot Dog. His Sausage and Onions were knocked to the floor by this lad climbing over. Shay picked up the Sausage and threw it right at this lad. It was harder to miss, but miss him he did. The lad dived to the floor and picked up the Hot Dog and held it cockily in his hand like a Top Boy holding a shooter! If this was a Morricone movie then there would be close ups of the pugilist's eyes, then the Hot Dog, then the eyes, then the onions, then a copper who had witnessed the whole thing and did the biggest eye roll you've ever seen and may even have muttered 'for fuck sake'. Entertainment was thin on the ground.

No longer in L Stand, I wandered nomadically around the ground, always with plenty of space around me. It was in one of these games in the second half of the season that I first came across Red Issue. I had heard of other clubs having fanzines but this was the first United one I had seen (although Red News was actually the first and still going strong after over 30 years). Having bought the programme religiously (for the token) every week it made a nice change to have something else to read. Unlike the programme however, Red Issue did not tow the company line and had no problem in complaining about and taking the piss out of the players who were underperforming and the chairman who held the purse strings. Red Issue was fucking hilarious and I loved it. I do remember getting the second issue at home to Everton late in the season. A 2-1 defeat in front of about 23,000 I barely remember the game as I was pissing myself at Red Issue and passing it to Shay to read what was making me laugh so much.

We decided there and then that we must get a letter published in the first edition of next season. I can't really remember much what was in it other than that it was irreverent, daft and funny. As we had both come up with ideas (I think my Dad even chipped in) then we needed a 'nom de plume' for this collective. That's when The Tom Sloan Appreciation Society was born. Tom Sloan was an average player from the late 70's/early 80's. Hailing from Ballymena his biggest claim to fame in a United shirt was playing in a game vs Ipswich away in 1980. We lost 6-0. Three weeks later I was in Stretford Arndale (a shopping centre twinned with The Walking Dead) when I spotted Tom Sloan and he became the first ever Manchester United player whose autograph I got. I remember the date as it was The Centenary Derby the next day.

Fast forward to the opening day of the 89/90 season. An incredible 4-1 win vs Champions Arsenal, Michael Knighton juggling his balls, Neil Webb with a debut worldie and more importantly, our letter was published. I had the bug now and sent another letter and an article the following month, both of which were published. The pattern continued and I would look forward to a new issue coming out each month to see if I was in it. A bit like Gary Numan jettisoned Tubeway Army, I had dumped Dad and Shay and had gone solo now to release *Cars,* but also because it was funny as fuck. I had noticed that the main guys who stood on Warwick Road selling the fanzine were cockneys and it was at Carrow Road, Norwich that I first nervously approached them before another shit away defeat. I knew the Editors had the names Veg and Zar and sure enough it was them, Chris and John to be precise, and they were very pleased to meet me.

"How do you fancy your own column?" they asked followed by the magic words "We will pay you of course". Jesus I must have been unbearable on that coach journey home! And so it was that The TSAS had a regular spot on the inside back page and I was clearing a Bullseye (£50) for every edition. One of the undoubted perks was not having to pay for a Jim Leighton condom T Shirt. I also persuaded them to throw in another one so I could give it to Paul and try and get in his good books.

Veg lived in Gorse Hill so I would pop round to his house to pick up a cheque for my column and hang out. He moved back to London for work so I had to find them after the match and get paid out of the takings so usually I was weighed down with change. One of these occasions was after the Derby in April 92. It was a disappointing 1-1 draw, especially with City having had a player sent off. I hung back and got my pocket full of coins (especially useful as I had a Wembley trip a few days later) and by the time I was heading back up Warwick Road, the city fans had just been let out and I was right in the middle of them. Thankfully I didn't have any colours on so it shouldn't be a problem. We shuffled along slowly like cattle and boy were the city fans happy

"You couldn't beat Ten Men!" they sang,

"The only football team to come from Manchester!" I just smiled and nodded along.

"Who's that lying on the runway!" Err, no and then I spotted it... coming from the direction of the buses on Chester Road where the United fans were singing their barbed responses came a pie... a Meat and Potato pie it transpires... I know this because from the moment I saw it, I knew it was going to hit me right in the fucking mush! Me, the only United fan out of hundreds of blues there! Everyone turned to see me wearing this pie and they were angry! They were angry for me! That's when I realised I had to be a blue for that moment and that's when I shouted it...

"You fucking Munich Bastards!" They roared their approval! "You don't even come from Manchester!"

"Yes mate you tell em!" I kept my head down then all the way back to the Norweb Club where Darren was waiting with a pint and he said

"I see you've brought your own pie". Funny bastard.

The TSAS column ran until the end of the 93 season when I couldn't really commit to writing a column when (spoiler alert!) I had stopped going to the match. Rest assured, Red Issue lived on as someone called Pete Boyle took over my spot on the inside back page. Not sure what became of him?

14. THE MAN WHOSE HEAD EXPANDED

After leaving St Bede's with only an English Language GCSE I had to resit my exams at South Trafford College. After the Dickensian Diatribe of Bede's it was a godsend to go to a college where you didn't need a uniform, weren't called by your Surname, only had to catch one Bus and, to boot, there were girls there! I also became a bit too familiar with The Pelican pub over the road, sometimes when I should have been in lessons but I did marginally better, getting Maths, Sociology and Media Studies but where too now?

After realising I was never going to be a Footballer, I hoped my next career path was in Journalism. However, every careers night lay out a road map of A Levels and University which clearly I wasn't on so I needed a leg up if it was ever going to happen.

After selling Burglar Alarms in St Helens for a couple of weeks, I spotted an advert for Editorial Messengers at the Manchester Evening News. Basically a copy boy/errand boy/tea boy whatever you wanted to call it but it was a rung on the ladder. I went for the interview and got the job which I was ecstatic about, if a little apprehensive. My Dad gave me a pep talk along the lines of

"Keep your head down and for Gods sake, don't tell them about all that 'Hurdy Gurdy' music that you listen to." His thought being that if I told them I liked The Stone Roses then I would have the DEA swooping down on the building. This misapprehension that I was Howard Marks wasn't helped by Paul planting some Drugs in my room. I came home from college to be greeted with my Dad and Pat holding about half a dozen little bags of powder that they had found on top of my wardrobe. I hadn't so much as smoked a cigarette in my life but they were convinced that these drugs were mine because I had a middle parting and listened to "The Harpurheys" as my Dad genuinely called The Happy Mondays. I pleaded my innocence but wasn't believed of course, just like I wasn't believed when I told them Paul was sticking his Dick in my face and making me sniff his Bell End. That sounds ridiculous but that's how it was. Naturally I didn't take up the planted drugs with Paul because I was scared of him. Did my Dad really believe it was me or was he scared of him too?

I suppose my musical tastes were a bit different. The first single I ever bought was *'Sgt Rock'* by XTC and the first album *'Kings of the Wild Frontier'* by Adam and the Ants. In fact I went to the St Monica's School Garden Party in 1981 with white insulation tape across my nose and I felt like the bees fucking knees. Still my music was frowned upon at home. I made the mistake of playing The Smiths downstairs once and my opera loving Step Mum was having none of it and put Classic FM back on. I also had to be careful about what Paul heard me listening to because he would break it down into minute details, probably because of his weed induced Paranoia. I once went off brand and bought a copy of *'An Innocent Man'* by Billy Joel. He called me a faggot and punched it until it broke in half.

I was hardly John Peel but I listened to my Dad anyway when I started work and played a very straight bat and just said I liked U2. I'm not lying there by the way, I'm unapologetic in saying I have always loved U2 and they put on a ruddy good live show! Luckily for me, within a week of starting I met two of my very best mates to this day in Chris and Barrie, and they liked The Wedding Present! The Smiths! New Order! Half Man Half Biscuit! You get the picture. They are also two of the funniest people I've ever met. Chris is pretty much my co-scriptwriter when it comes to the one liners whereas Barrie had a surreal sense of humour that I really bought into and is the funniest man I have ever met. It's no surprise that the three of us got very heavily into Vic and

Bob when *'Big Night Out'* came out.

Chris lived in Great Moor and was the only person I knew who had Sky. He also had very cool parents in Big Chris and Sheila plus his Sister Nicola was lovely too. It was nothing like what me and Barrie were used to at home and we used to love going there for the weekend. We went there one Friday Night to the George and Dragon (we liked it there because it had *"Kennedy"* by The Wedding Present on the Jukebox) and then the meat market that was The Bamboo Night Club. On Saturday, the two Chris's were going to Wembley to watch Stockport County play Stoke and we were told to 'let ourselves out' when we were ready. But neither me nor Barrie wanted to go home. He had Sky TV and a dartboard, and Sky TV! Plus it was England vs Brazil the next day which we wanted to watch (you can guess the channel). The day got later and later, we watched the County match and started to think of more ridiculous reasons to stay including getting in bed together and letting them accidentally catch us!

I absolutely loved the job at the Evening News and would leave 'Phil's gag of the day' by the clocking in machine and it wasn't just the Messengers who were laughing at my jokes. I worked on the Features section. Not quite the cut and thrust of Newsdesk but this was The Summer of Madchester! The Diary section was being asked to run more and more stories about The Roses, Afflecks Palace, Hacienda etc and would ask for our input. Before I could speak, Barrie would pipe up with

"Madchester is shit! Listen to The Fall!"

Another one of the cooler guys who worked there was Terry Christian. He would give you the time of day for starters and then we found out we were both Reds and both ex-Bede's. We would sit on a bench on Spinningfield and chuck pennies where the people were waiting to cross the road on Deansgate and laugh as they all panicked thinking they had lost money. I think he told that story when he was on Wogan. Unfortunately my possessions didn't do very well when Terry was about. One night a few of us were in The Tommy Ducks pub near G Mex, famed for its knickers on the wall. Barrie had leant Terry some Captain Beefheart vinyl or something and he had a pre-release copy of *Extricate* by The Fall on tape. So we all sat taking it in turns to listen to Telephone Thing, Hilary, Bill is Dead etc. Only problem was that Tel hit the Stop button a little too vigorously and the Play button came flying off! We couldn't find the little bugger anywhere! (The button, not Christian). Another time we were talking about which teachers were still at Bede's from his day and I said I would bring in a copy of my school photo which I had rolled up in a tube so he could see if Mr Stienne still looked like Bjorn from ABBA. He took it home with him for a good look but never came back. He had got a new job as a presenter on a programme called The Word. That's Showbiz!

15. SON OF A FATHER

So after the crazy opening day win over Arsenal, things didn't go well. Fergie backed up the £2M spent on Webb and Phelan with another £2M on Paul Ince, £1M on Danny Wallace and a British Record £2.3M on Gary Pallister. Given the British Record now is £100M for Jack Grealish then this is the equivalent of a £300M spend now.

After promising wins over Millwall and Portsmouth in which both Ince and Wallace scored, the next port of call was Manchester City for the first Derby Match in 3 years and my first visit to Maine Road. I took my place and stood on a bench in Platt Lane and things were ok for about 5 minutes. Then the game had to be stopped for some serious mither in North Stand with United fans popping up all over the place and being marched round the pitch. All very exciting stuff! Sadly that's where the excitement ended as City absolutely battered us 5-1. Not just did the United fans sing Ferguson Out but sang the name of Tommy Docherty! I sat with my Uncle Danny who saw the world through red tinted spectacles and believed we would have won if the game hadn't stopped after 5 minutes. This is as bad as saying 'well at least we scored the best goal of the game'. The natives were restless and I had an article printed in Red Issue which was along the lines of;

FERGIE'S CHIPPY

CHIPS	£1
FISH	£2
PUDDINGS	£2.3M

There were a few more, Steve Bruce Hoof Cakes, Donaghy Kebabs etc but you get the point. Years later I read an interview with Pally where he said the early days were difficult and there was a joke in one of the local fanzines about Fergies Chippy and we all laughed at that and passed it round the dressing room. That was my article! In 2012 I went to see Pallister do an After Dinner speech in Ashton and when it came to the Q and A section, I asked him if he remembered it.

"Oh yeah I do, that was really funny. It wasn't you that wrote it was it?'

Gulp "Yeah, it was actually." Surprised he returned

"Oh right, err thanks a lot pal."

"Well to be fair, you were shit at the time Gary!"

A gasp filled the room... followed by absolute bedlam and laughter! Pally took it very well and didn't kill me when I asked for a picture later. It could have gone very wrong though!

Fergie was really under pressure and the defeat at home to Crystal Palace in early December will always be remembered as the 'Ta Ra Fergie' game. In amongst the boos and catcalls, a bed sheet was being waved about in J Stand. It read 'Ta Ra Fergie. 3 years of excuses and still crap'. We talked about it in The Norweb Club after the game and my Dad knew exactly who was responsible. Pete Molyneux worked with my Dad at Norweb and was given a right dressing down by my old man on the Monday. You don't air your dirty laundry in public... or your bedsheets!

Another bonus working at the Evening News was that there were other match going reds there in Chris, Leon and Pete and soon we decided to go to the away games together too. The MEN Away club didn't get off to the best start

CHARLTON ATHLETIC (AT SELHURST PARK) LOST 2-0
ARSENAL (AT HIGHBURY) LOST 1-0

LIVERPOOL (AT ANFIELD) DREW 0-0
ASTON VILLA (AT VILLA PARK) LOST 3-0

This Villa game stood out for two reasons. Firstly when we got to Old Trafford on that cold Boxing Day morning (kick off in Birmingham was 12 noon) the gates to the Scoreboard Paddock were still open from when the players had parked their cars there. A few of us wandered in and straight onto the pitch. Sadly no one had a football so we all had to pretend living our dream and scoring at The Theatre of Dreams…just without a ball. The second thing was a helicopter hovering over the ground throughout the game and at one point a booming Brummie voice came out of the chopper

"Oi you on Witton Lane! Step away from the cowin' car or you're nicked!"

Four games and no goals scored and our next fixture is probably the most famous 3rd Round tie we have ever played and the beginning of the most extraordinary cup run.

16.   SUNDAY BLOODY SUNDAY

**3rd Round. Sunday January 7th 1990.
Nottingham Forest (A)**

I had never known a game with such certainty about it. If United lost then Fergie would be sacked. There were even people who wanted the reds to lose so that Fergie would go. The game was Live on BBC1 so it felt like a national public execution.

The Red Army travelled in their thousands including the full complement of the Evening News Travel Club. The Reds were not at full strength with Blackmore and Beardsmore both playing in the midfield. Even Ralphie made it onto the bench. Backed by the vociferous away support, United took the lead from a stooping header courtesy of Mark Robins. The goal was reminiscent of Jimmy Greenhoff's goal against Liverpool at Goodison Park in 1979.

Forest got stronger and it looked like they were going to break through. A hopeful ball was lobbed into the area and Jim Leighton came out with a feeble punch and the ball was steered home by Nigel Clough. I remember vividly almost trying to run through people to get at Leighton whilst I screamed obscenities at him. Then I spotted the offside flag and it was greeted like a second goal! A definite 'I was there' game.

**4th Round. Sunday January 28th 1990.
Hereford United (A)**

We had lost both games between these two games so we had hardly kicked on from the Forest one. Me and Chris got on the coach at Old Trafford when the driver announced

"We have no idea if the game is going ahead due to torrential rain, so we may get turned around and come home at any point". Oh fuck.

The closer to Hereford we got the wetter it became, but we knew the closer we got then the more likely that the game would go ahead. We got to within a mile of the stadium and there was a football pitch that you could barely see the goals… they were underwater! There was no way this was going ahead!

The car park we were supposed to go to was waterlogged so we parked up and had to climb through a cattle market (Tits and Hangovers… to be explained later) to get to the ground. This wasn't the only cattle based shenanigans as before the game, a Bull was led around the pitch. Fans of Blue Peter will be glad to know that it did shit on the pitch.

Finally we were in and stood behind the goal and it was without doubt the most scared I had felt at a game. The terrace was quite a way back away from the pitch with a 'moat' betwixt the two. Normally people would be in the moat as well but the torrential rain meant everyone crammed into the terrace. Hughes volleyed one wide (I would have scored it) and the surge of the crowd lifted us off our feet. I'm taller than Chris so he couldn't see a thing and we agreed to relocate to the moat. Although we got soaked, we felt safe and couldn't really see the other end of the pitch where Clayton Blackmore scuffed a late uninspired winner.

5th Round. Sunday February 18th 1990. Newcastle United (A)

Newcastle were a Second Division team at this time. No sign of Keegan yet, I think Jim Smith was in charge. Even St James's Park was unrecognisable as we stood on a very small terrace on what seemed to be a building site. The game however was a cracker.

Robins scored to give us a Half Time lead but Newcastle came back and when they scored, half of the stand came on the pitch with them. Wallace put us back in front but back came The Toon and the pitch invasion. Finally Brian McClair scored his first goal since the 80's to give us the win. This time the pitch invasion got as far as our 18 yard box and it looked like there was going to be a rumble but thankfully the Geordie Po Po kept them at bay. It was probably Spender.

6th Round. Sunday 11th March 1990. Sheffield United (A)

Another away draw and another Sunday game but we were really starting to smell the Hot Dogs of Wembley. Sheff U were another Second Division team that we were confident of dispatching. My Uncle Danny came with me to this one. We sat in the seats whilst Chris stood below us. This was to be the first of 5 trips I would make to Bramhall Lane in the space of 3 Years (Won 2 Lost 3).

I liked having Danny with us. He was a very softly spoken hairdresser with more than a whiff of Lavender about him. However once the whistle went he was a man possessed. Swearing, whistling, very passionate and very very funny. On the coach to the game we were crossing 'The Snake Pass' when Danny showed me a spot where if you were lucky, you got to see the steam from the railway track below. I think he still thought it was the 50's.

The Reds won easily and were far better value than the 1-0 scoreline. The Draw for the semi final had been kind and we had avoided Liverpool who were going for the Double having just missed out on it the two previous years. We drew yet another Second Division team. The Scousers could wait until Wembley.

17. THIS IS HOW IT FEELS

Semi Final. Sunday 8th April 1990. Oldham Athletic (N)

I was very excited for my first FA Cup Semi Final. The big occasion had brought out the big guns and Dad and Shay came along to their first away games since the 85 Final. For the first time, both semi finals were to be shown Live on BBC1 on the same day which meant we got to watch the first semi final in the pub. It was Half Time when we got to The Whitworth, a very small pub about ten minutes walk from Maine Road and Liverpool were 1-0 up. The Second Half and subsequent extra time were absolutely breathless as Crystal Palace scored in the first and last minute of the Second Half and the score finished 3-3. Dancing knobhead Alan Pardew came up with the Palace winner in Extra Time! I hadn't celebrated in a pub so much since Michael Thomas had scored against Liverpool the season before to win the league for Arsenal. Of course with every goal came another pint and we were absolutely steaming by the end of the game and because of Extra Time, didn't have very long to get to our game which had almost been forgotten about. As my eyes adjusted to the sunlight coming out of the pub, I could see that someone had daubed on a wall…

"PALACE 4 LFC 3. NO SCOUSE AT WEMBLEY!"

Now for our semi final vs Oldham Athletic. Shay and I were very low down behind the goal in the North Stand at Maine Road and you could see how pissed I was when I appeared on the telly as Latics took the lead after just 5 minutes. They should have won the game! Marshall ran the bollocks off Bruce and Pallister at the back. Earl Barrett had Hughes in his pocket and Jim Leighton looked absolutely lost in goal. They had clearly worked out that Jim wasn't very good at crosses and was constantly scurrying back across his goal with the ball sailing to the on rushing strikers. We also had Robson and Webb both returning in midfield after lengthy injuries.

This was too much for me to take. I was absolutely bladdered, my head was banging and my Wembley dream looked like it was in tatters. Thankfully the returning Robson and Webb both managed to score and the second semi final of the day spilled into Extra Time. 2-2 soon became 3-3 and Oldham had chances to win it. We were grateful for the second chance.

Semi Final Replay Wednesday 11th April 1990. Oldham Athletic (N)

Shouldn't this be on a Sunday? One of the perks of working at the Evening News is that you got to go and 'check the phones' that David Meek (United) or Peter Gardener (City) would dial in their match report for the Pink Final. I got to check the phones this day so got a taxi from The Evening News at Spinningfield to Maine Road. I was led to the tunnel and then up into the press box. I found the Evening News phone and dialled back to the Sports Desk. Once they established it was working I just sat there for a while looking round at the ground and thinking I will be back here in a few hours. Walking back down the tunnel when I spotted the Manager's Office with the door open. I kind of leant into it as I walked past and saw that Howard Kendall was nowhere to be seen. I went into the office. My heart was pumping as I looked at a big year planner (next to his Everton calendar) and a tactics board. I considered moving it around or taking a shit on his desk but settled with waving my fist at his desk and shouting blue cunts!

More civilised pre-game drinkies in a pub called The Denmark (don't bother looking for it. It's not there anymore). A mate of my Dad's called Pete Sharman was there with his Daughter Rachel, who I definitely fancied. Having dazzled her with the news that I was the man behind The TSAS, I stood up to go to the loo and went straight into the ladies. Smooooth.

I was in the North Stand again for the replay but up in the corner. The marvellous architecture of Maine Road struck again as despite purchasing both seats together, there was a girder between us so we weren't actually sat together. Robson was magnificent and although Oldham were still dangerous we had more control than the Sunday. It took extra time to settle it as Mark Robins kept up his excellent record in the cup and slid home the winner. It may seem strange looking back now at an FA Cup Semi vs a lower league side being treated with such euphoria but this was a massive moment. Now for the final.

FA Cup Final Saturday 12th May 1990. Crystal Palace (N)

And so to my first FA Cup Final. My Dad had sat with Uncle Danny for the two semis but Danny decided he didn't want to go to Wembley because his record there was so bad! He had been half a dozen times and we lost every game! Dad and Danny's Season Tickets meant they were guaranteed tickets and the rest of us had to scramble with our token sheets. I put forward that the spare ticket should go to Chris as he had been to every round so far but our 'tour of duty' in the moat at Hereford counted for nothing and Dad decided the spare ticket should go to Paul. Oh joy.

Like my previous Wembley trips we went on the train and found ourselves in a pub called The Fusilier. A few pints were had and then a few Palace fans spilled in singing *'Glad All Over'* and challenging any United fan to sing the official Cup Final song (the turgid *'We Will Stand Together'*). By now we were sitting outside and just as the atmosphere was getting a little moody, a big gust of wind came and blew my Dad's 'Maxi size' packet of Salt and Vinegar Seabrooks off the table and onto the floor. "Me fucking crisps" he desperately cried as they blew away and everybody pissed themselves at this. Rumble avoided!

The game itself was almost a carbon copy of the first semi final as Palace seemed far more up for it but incapable of putting United away. Just like Oldham did, they targeted Jim Leighton and he was at fault with two of the Palace goals and got away with a lot more. Thanks to a couple from Hughes and one from Robson we managed to salvage a 3-3 draw after a sapping Extra Time and my Red Issue Jim Leighton condom T Shirt had never looked more apt. On the walk back to the train station I stopped at a phone box and rang my Mum, asking if she could buy my ticket for the replay as an early 18th Birthday present and thankfully she did.

***FA Cup Final Replay Thursday 17th May 1990.
Crystal Palace (N)***

Dad decided not to go to the final so I thought Chris might have a chance again. However this time 'Dad' decided that Paul's Girlfriend Karen should have the ticket and that they would use the Season Tickets too. I say it was my Dad's decision but it was clearly my Step Mum Pat who decided this one. Shay and I had both been to every Home game that season and I had also been to every game of this cup run, nearly all of which had been on a Sunday and away from home. I could understand Dad calling dibs on the guaranteed tickets for the game he was going to, but to give Paul and Karen the tickets and leave me and Shay having to queue overnight with Token Sheets was ridiculous and Dad knew that. It was just another example of the favouritism that Paul received. Years later when I would go to my Dad and Pat's Caravan in Caernarfon, there would be pictures of Pat's

Grandchildren all over, but never my Dad's.

The journey down was pretty forgettable. Paul made me buy him a Pint of Cider with the last of my money in The Imperial near Piccadilly Station but that's about it. The big question on everyone's lips would be whether Fergie would drop his long standing goalkeeper Jim Leighton in favour of the on loan Les Sealey. We got our answer just before kick off when a visibly crumpled Leighton had to walk to his seat on the bench, wearing his United suit. Sealey was in! Palace tried to intimidate him but Mad Les was made of sterner stuff and we won a moribund final 1-0, courtesy of Lee Martin. United players celebrated and the more astute would have noticed that a lot of the squad were wearing Morson International caps. Apparently Jim McGregor had been slipped a few quid to make sure that the players were wearing the caps if we won and Jim sure delivered.

The real drama was with the Goalkeepers though. The story goes that after the match, Sealey gave Leighton his winners medal, saying he had only played in one game and didn't deserve it. Leighton quietly slipped it back into Sealey's pocket at the party afterwards. Leighton only played once more for United and has never spoken to Ferguson since. He did however strike up a relationship with Sealey and when Les suddenly passed away in 2002, Leighton was one of the pall bearers at his funeral. This one, he didn't drop.

18. LIKE AN ANGEL

I loved working at the Manchester Evening News. The job was a doddle, I liked my work colleagues and I was in the right place at the right time. Like most Mancunians my age, I liked The Stone Roses and The Happy Mondays and I was right at the epicentre of the Second Summer of Love or Madchester as it was known. Dave Broad was another Messenger who was a big Roses fan and wore flared jeans that could drown Wiltshire. He was a good lad for a Blue was Broady and as well as our Friday Night sessions after work, we went to watch Lancashire in the One Day Cricket (with Baz) and we went to Bury to see the poets, Henry Normal and John Hegley.

A messenger's life was a short one, you only worked there until your 18th Birthday and then left unless they liked the cut of your jib and kept you on. So imagine how delighted I was when I was summoned to HR and asked to stay on as a Messenger 'until the right role came along'. They had received good feedback from the guys on the Features floor where I worked and were also impressed with my work on Red Issue. I may have exaggerated my part in its creation and they certainly weren't aware that I was liberating photos from the Picture Library. The trick to pinching pictures was to request a genuine file and the one you wanted. So you would often see requests for Nicolae Ceaucescu and Morrissey, Princess Anne and Mudhoney etc.

It was also the Summer of Love as I fell for a fellow messenger. Rhona worked on The Guardian side of the building so any interactions were usually in the canteen at lunch time. Other people started to notice that we were timing our breaks to be at the same time. We made each other laugh and she liked The Mighty Lemon Drops which was pretty cool. One weekend I was looking after my Mum's Dog and we spent two hours on the phone. If only it wasn't for her pesky Boyfriend!

It was also Italia 90 of course and the opening game classic between Argentina and Cameroon happened to be my 18th birthday and I had a really good turn out (including Rhona) in The Old Nag's Head to watch it and then onto Brahms and Liszt. The Nags and The Sawyers were our pubs of choice and we watched lots of World Cup games there.

Then late in July there was a spate of redundancies announced and I got a letter from HR. I was to finish the following week as it looked like my future role was gone before I could even start it. I was devastated. In fact it was *'Twisting My Melon Man!'* And it looked like I wouldn't be Twisting any Melons anytime soon.

Having watched United play at Bury on the Wednesday night and having played snooker with Broady on the Thursday, my leaving do was on the Friday. Everyone signed my shirt and Rhona wrote that she did not have Thighs like Mark Hughes followed by lots of love hearts. We danced the night away and I kicked myself for not trying to instigate any shenanigans. Would I even see her again?

Of course I was now out of work and Marie said that there was a job at her place, a Plant Hire Company called M&H based at Trafford House overlooking God's little acre. I had an interview with a guy called Steve Grundy who asked why I wanted this job as a cash hire clerk. I told him I wanted to get back into Journalism and this was a stopgap until I found something, plus it would be cool to work with my Sister. He appreciated my honesty and gave me the job there and then. This was a relief as I now had a short term job to pay for Football and Gigs. I worked there for 25 years.

Meanwhile back on Love Island, Rhona rang me the following Friday and said a few were going to see *'Gremlins 2'* after work at the ABC (now The Moon Under Water) and would I like to come. We shared a coke with two straws for fucks sake, surely

I wouldn't blow it this time! When the film finished, I offered to walk her back to her Bus Stop and this time there was some serious snogging in the shadow of the 192 stop! Over the next couple of weeks we would meet up for dinner which was lovely. She asked me if I would like to go to 21 Piccadilly with her on Friday Night on a double date with a friend of hers. I was made up although there were a couple of problems. This fell in the same week as two big awayers. On the Wednesday I was going to Glasgow with Pete to watch United play at Rangers and on the Saturday I was in London for the Charity Shield (the traditional curtain raiser to the English Season) vs Liverpool. I had also never been in 21 Piccadilly but had heard about their strict ID policy and I was only 18.

I went to Rangers on a coach which set on fire somewhere near Carlisle! Astonishingly having 'cooled down for Half an Hour' we got back on and completed our journey. We sat amongst the Rangers fans and kept our cool when Russell Beardsmore scored the game's only goal. We didn't look quite so cool when we 'doubled up' at Last Orders only for the bar staff to come and pick them up at 11pm. In Glasgow, last orders meant leave the pub now!

I still had my ID dilemma and was going to have to ask Paul if I could borrow his driving licence. It might leave me in his debt but I couldn't think what else to do. By the way Rhona was a year younger than me but I just assumed all girls had fake ID. Paul came up trumps on the understanding that I would be home from Wembley in time to watch the Nigel Benn fight on the Saturday. I made it into the club and had a really good night. There were no stolen kisses, it was full on smooching and I'd never felt so relaxed. I'd also never paid £2 for a pint before lol. Her friend also worked at the Evening News and I got the impression I had been talked about as she told me that Rhona definitely liked me.

I woke up the next morning with loads of 21 Piccadilly doilies on my snooker table. No idea how that happened! I sneaked into Paul's room to drop off the drivers licence and his girlfriend was sleeping on her back with the boobies out. Small victories! I had a great trip to Wembley (I went with Chris and Pete) and had a few scoops in The Green Man. The game finished 1-1 (Blackmore) and the Charity Shield (TTCRTTES) was shared. I was feeling the pace of a crazy few weeks now and as we approached Stockport, I couldn't even bear the thought of trying to get back to Urmston in time for the fight so I asked Chris if I could stay at his. We got in just in time for the fight and Benn won to become World Champion. When the fight finished, I rang home to tell them I was staying out and to speak to Paul about the fight. He loved boxing and Nigel Benn was his favourite fighter and I was genuinely buzzing he had won. Paul was fucking fuming. Where was I? I had promised. I had spoiled the moment. I tried to tell him that I didn't drive the train and it wasn't my fault it took so long to get home but he was having none of it. I knew I would have to face the music the next day when I got home.

Few people will remember the bruise that came up in my first week of my new job at M&H. I said that the train had braked suddenly and I banged into a door. I was even sounding like an abuse victim now.

19. SHALL WE TAKE A TRIP?

After the FA Cup triumph we got the exciting news that the European ban was being lifted meaning we could compete in the European Cup Winners Cup and there was much excitement when Pecsi Munkas rolled into town. United spared no expense and released balloons from a giant pair of bollocks on the pitch. Goals from Blackmore and Webb saw off the Hungarians and maybe taking the day off to watch the Second Leg with Barrie in The Old Nags Head was a bit excessive but it was still a good all-dayer, ending in Piccadilly Snooker Centre where we saw Alex Higgins fall off a Snooker Table. I didn't ask for his autograph this time.

The Second Round Draw was a bit closer to home and me and Chris looked forward to our first Euro awayer in Wrexham. They all count! We had started our away trip journey in short sleeves at Sunderland but it was freezing cold in this strange foreign land. In between those two awayers was our first Maine Road Derby since 5-1. We were to be standing on Kippax corner this time and it was also Chris's 18th Birthday. The early kick off time ruled out the pub so me and Darren had a plan. A new Victoria Wine was opening near me and we fathomed that if we were the very first customers when it opened at 10am then there would be freebies! Sadly there was no ribbon cutting ceremony or free beers, so we bought a few cans and got on the 22 to the ground anyway. We saved one for Chris to have his first birthday drink out of a can of warm Boddies smooth. It looked like this Derby was going the way of the season before as City raced into a 2-0 and then 3-1 lead. Two late goals from Brian McClair brought utter pandemonium in the United End and it finished 3-3.

The week after the Derby we played Arsenal at home, losing 1-0 but the game was remembered for a 21 man brawl between the players. Both teams were eventually docked points and eyebrows were raised when the two sides were drawn together in the next round of the Rumbelows Cup. I definitely wanted to go to this one (imagine wanting to go to a League Cup away game!) and was definitely regretting the Pecsi Munkas Day Off as I had none left and would have to be back at work the next morning. One of the benefits of working next to the ground was that it made it nice and easy to catch the Coach to Away games from outside The Dog and Partridge and this time it was myself, Pete and his two mates Tim and Jock. We got to North London at about 4.30 and took refuge in The Drayton Park pub. This was United. This was life. There was no better feeling than singing in the pub with your mates before the game, even more so away from home. I remember the Landlord getting lairy with some reds and next minute The Old Bill are there shutting the place down! We just found another pub. I think it was called The Highbury Barn but it was full of Arsenal and they didn't expect this Northern Invasion. Eventually we got to our seats and they announced there would be a 10 minute delay to kick off. Pint? Why not!

Now I must have thought that I had one too many because after Blackmore had given us an early lead ("80 seconds!") we got another from Hughes just before Half Time. Arsenal were unbeaten and didn't concede many so we were happy with this when fuck me old boots Lee Sharpe made it 3-0! Its raining goals at Highbury! We were in dream land now and then the Half Time scores were announced and it was Coventry City 4 Nottingham Forest 4. This definitely made me think I was tripping. Little did I know that 200 miles away my Dad was varnishing the floor and had the same thought as the varnish could give you hallucinations. Two quick Arsenal goals had us panicking a bit but the rampant reds were having none of it. Lee Sharpe was having the night of his life and followed up his first half Thunder Twat with a neat header for 4-2 and then an assured right foot finish for his Hat Trick. Needs to work on his celebration though.

Danny Wallace completed the scoring for an incredible 6-2 win at Highbury. This remains by far my favourite ever United away game. On Saturday we were all present again, only this time at Goodison Park as Lee Sharpe scored again for a 1-0 win and The Sharpie Shuffle was born!

I had my worst ever hangover at a match at Highfield Road, Coventry and really could have done without us scoring early or getting a last minute equaliser. There were a lot of hangovers on the coach down to our next trip, Spurs on New Year's Day. This time the 5pm kick off time worked in our favour for a bit of shut eye between the drinking! For reasons I never knew, the Red Issue Coach had received an invite to a Spurs Social Club before the game, probably from their fanzine. This place was cavernous and plenty of Hair of the Dog was being had. In true cockney style there was someone playing the Old Joanna and although not quite Chas and Dave, they were singing Spurs songs. A few Reds tried to get some United songs going which didn't go down too well with the locals. We needed a packet of my Dad's crisps to blow away in the wind but in their absence I had a moment of inspiration. I dived on the piano and played something I had learned just days earlier on my Baby Niece Becki's play piano she got for Christmas... I played *'Step on'* by The Happy Mondays! The Reds cheered! Melons were twisted! Tables were overturned! I wish I could have followed up by playing for more than 10 seconds but I decided that The Spurs Social Club wasn't ready yet for Chopsticks.

Spurs scored early but just like the season before, Steve Bruce scored a penalty. The season before we were there to see Gazza run rings around us. Since then he had took Italia 90 by storm and was the biggest personality in the country and still a fucking incredible footballer. Therefore we celebrated like a goal when he was sent off for dissent in the Second Half, and then we got to celebrate a goal as Brian McClair popped up with a last minute winner! What a start to 1991... and it was going to get better.

20.   DALLIANCE

And what of Rhona? After our blissful night in 21 Piccadilly she went on holiday to Greece. I was worried I would be forgotten about instantly but I did receive a Postcard which was awesome. On the day she got home we arranged to go to the pictures (The Odeon now as the ABC was having a few extra floors added ready to become Wetherspoons toilets) to see Memphis Belle. I say we saw Memphis Belle but I'm definitely the only one who did as the flight home caught up with her and she fell asleep. I assume it was that and not bored of my lame attempt at doing the popcorn bucket trick (joke).

Then things just went quiet. The drinks in town became less frequent. A date to see Another 48 Hours was made then later cancelled. Broady came to Anfield with us (despite being a blue) and no doubt enjoyed Beardsley's Hat Trick and a 4-0 win for the Dippers. When I asked him what was going on he just said 'she was going through a tough time at the moment' and if I rang the office to talk to her, they would say that she wasn't in. I got the feeling it was nothing to do with me *per se*.

Finally after a few weeks it was someone's leaving do and we were in The Old Nags Head, upstairs in the pool room. There were still no Public Displays of Affection because as far as I knew, she still had a boyfriend. It seemed awkward. She was talking to someone else and Broady came back from the bar and passed Rhona her drink. She took it without looking at him or acknowledging him. I knew there and then. I tried to tell myself it couldn't be, but I was kidding myself.

Later that week, Broady rang me at work and asked if I fancy a pint afterwards. Not an uncommon occurrence at the time. Pretty much straight away he told me he had a new bird.

"Oh right, anyone from work?" I asked from behind a metaphorical sofa. He shrugged his shoulders and said

"Sorry pal. You know how it is," You may think I was angry at him but do you know what, I wasn't. It can't have been easy for him coming to tell a mate that the girl he was sweet on, was now his Girlfriend but he did. I thanked him for being honest and just said I would have to settle for beating him at pool.

Let's not get carried away, I would have far more meaningful, loving and proper relationships as I got older. In fact you couldn't even call it a relationship, just stolen kisses and a couple of dates. But this was 'The Second Summer of Love', the Summer of Madchester and I was right at the heart of it. Be it Afflecks, Eastern Bloc, The Hac, The Strangeway Riots, working at the Manchester Evening News was a major ambition and now that had gone, the *Dalliance* with Rhona was me holding on to a whole magical time in my life that I could see slipping away. I had absolutely no right to feel any malice and I didn't. Or maybe that's because I have never been any good at confrontation. The years of abuse have left me unable to face difficult decisions or situations, I just bury my head in the sand and pretend it's not happening.

Happily, Barrie and Chris from the Evening News have remained friends for life. We have sunk endless pints, been to countless gigs and been there for each other through good times and bad. Thanks to the power of Facebook I have managed to make contact with a few of my fellow messengers. I did meet up with Pete (remember Arsenal 6-2) at a Grimes gig in 2012 (with the then soon to be 2nd Mrs Taylor) and chatted with both Broady and Leon, always promising that we must do that reunion we have always talked about.

I managed to find Rhona too. I just sent a Friend Request rather than a message as I was a bit nervous. Then I spotted a message in my inbox.

"Is that Phil as in Evening News Phil?"

"Well it's Philip actually but if you want me to be called Evening News Phil then that's fine". We got on really well. She was happily married (to a guy called Phil… arf!) and had a couple of grown up sons. She is a nurse now and messaged me when I was first trying to come to terms with Cluster Headaches.

I was online friends now with both Rhona and Broady, a situation I wouldn't have seen coming back in late 1990. Therefore it seemed quite apt that I was the one who told Rhona about Broady passing away. Barrie told me he had seen it on his status but clearly written by someone else informing his Friends of the terrible news. As far as I know it had come after a 'short illness' right at the height of the Pandemic. I don't know if it was Covid but it's a definite possibility. He was 47 and he was a good guy. I'm sorry we never went for that pint.

21. THE ONLY LIVING BOY IN NEW CROSS

United hadn't had a realistic crack at the League Title for a few years. They came second in 1988 but were miles behind Liverpool. They had become a Cup team and a very good one at that. The 1990 FA Cup Final was the first of 8 Cup Finals in 7 years.

Halifax were first up in The Rumbelows Cup and the highlights were Jim Leighton's last appearance and playing 4 full backs at Home. To Halifax! The 3rd Round Draw though saw us pitted against Champions Liverpool at Home on Halloween. It had only been a few weeks since they had beaten us 4-0 but we fancied ourselves against anybody under the lights at Old Trafford. These were the days when both teams still played their strongest teams in the League Cup and this game was no exception. United struck first with a Steve Bruce penalty. One of many that season.

One thing that Mark Hughes did enjoy was a good dust up with the Dippers. He had taken a bad knock to the ankle and looked like he was about to be substituted when he picked the ball up about 30 yards out, shrugged off a challenge and then hit a dipping, swerving shot that left Grobbelaar grasping thin air. Looking back you just hope there were no shenanigans going on from Grobbelaar. The atmosphere was incredible and went up a few degrees when Burrows chopped down Danny Wallace when clean through. 'OFF! OFF! OFF!' Chanted Uncle Danny. Did I mention he hated Liverpool (though not as much as he hated Arsenal). Lee Sharpe made the game safe and we won 3-1. No sooner had we got home for the highlights than the draw was made and we were rewarded for our endeavours with a draw away at unbeaten Arsenal (we read about that in Chapter 19).

Travelling home from Highbury and we heard on the radio that we had been drawn away at Southampton in the Quarter Final. The Saints had an exciting young striker called Alan Shearer leading their line and he said he based his game on Mark Hughes. He was certainly giving our back four a run for its money and was a master in shithousery and volleys like Hughes was and it was no surprise when he put Southampton in front. Hughes wasn't to be outdone though and hit a magnificent back post volley that Clive Tyldsley described as "Instinctive and unstoppable." Hughes was one of those players who scored his goals in clusters and then none for weeks. He had already scored in both rounds of the FA Cup vs QPR and Bolton and in the League Cup Quarter Final Replay it was Hughes 3 Shearer 2 as Sparky's Hat Trick trumped Chicken and Beans brace.

His scoring boots deserted him though as we were knocked out of the FA Cup away to Norwich City. Me and Chris made the 5,000 mile trip to Norwich on a Monday Night whilst normal people found the nearest pub that had a BSkyB Squarial. That was The Robin Hood in Stretford for my Dad and Brothers. My lasting memory of this game was with the clock approaching 90 minutes and Pallister already thrown up front, a bloke stood in front of us turned to his mate and said 'I got this coat dry cleaned last week. Guess how much?' Who gives a fuck! That was a long journey home and yes I did have work the next morning.

The draw for the semi final of The Rumbelows Cup had been delayed due to the start of the First Gulf War so I woke to find that another war was about to break out; we had drawn Leeds United. The first leg was played at a very frosty Old Trafford in the days when both legs were played on a Sunday afternoon on ITV. There was very much the feeling of 'work to do' as we ran out 2-1 winners and Lee Sharpe had destroyed Mel Sterland all afternoon. Since his Hat Trick vs Arsenal he had become the United poster boy and even broken into the England Team. Against Leeds he simply knocked it 30 yards in front of himself and Sterland didn't stand a chance. Chris and I went to the Second Leg at Elland Road, both going for the first time. I went there again another couple of times for League games and the trip down was always the same. The police would march us from the coaches, under a subway where both sets of fans would throw things at each other and then drop us at the door of the away terraces. However because this was a Cup game we had more tickets and we were sitting in the stand behind the goal but the Police had already left us. We had to run the gauntlet of the baying Leeds supporters who were pouring out of The Old Peacock pub towards us.

Halfway up the stand were a row of private boxes, the old fashioned type behind a glass window. For most games of course there would be Leeds United supporters in those seats but for this game it was Manchester United supporters and were giving them all sorts of abuse and throwing any discarded drinks at the windows. We sat right on the back row, in front of the private box belonging to the 'little funny one from The Grumbleweeds'. At first it was a bit light hearted as people recognised him (Graham Walker he was called). However it soon turned to abuse and after laughing it off for too long he reverted to type and started mimicking an airplane, a gesture mocking the Munich Air Disaster and red rag to a bull for United fans. They started throwing anything they could get their hands on at the box and the police soon stepped in to first warn The little Grumbleweed and then again to escort him from the premises! (By the way, he isn't the only Z list celebrity I saw do the Airplane gesture. I saw Vince Earl AKA Ron Dixon off Brookside do it once at Anfield).

On the pitch we were in a right battle. Leeds threw everything at United and Mal Donaghy in for the injured Bruce was having his best game for the reds. Sharpe still had the beating of Sterland and his pace was a real threat on the break. The game turned in the final two minutes, first Sealey made a magnificent save before McClair sent Sharpe away. He had the freedom of Elland

Road as he closed in on goal but seemed to have taken it too wide. From a tight angle however he drilled it home and we were in dreamland. Sharpie did his shuffle in front of the United fans to celebrate a 1-0 victory. We were kept in the ground for about an hour after the game and all we could hear were police sirens and helicopters as they tried to clear the Leeds supporters. We were going back to Wembley and I was off to find out how much it cost to dry clean a coat.

22. ONLY SHALLOW

The final was a huge anti-climax. After the titanic battles with Liverpool, Arsenal, Southampton and Leeds, it seemed like we just had to turn up against Championship side Sheffield Wednesday, even if they were managed by Big Ron. Unfortunately it seems like the players thought the same too.

Four of us went down on the coach. Myself, Shay, Chris and Darren and like the Charity Shield (the traditional curtain raiser to the English Season) we went to The Green Man before the game and all seemed well with the world. It was my fifth trip to Wembley in less than a year. Shay and I had come down for the American Football the previous August with my Brother in Law Bertie and a friend called Dave, and had stayed over in a B&B. The following day we went our separate ways for a bit of sightseeing and we had a wander down to Wembley to see if we could do the Tour. There wasn't a soul about and no sign of any tours. Shay then noticed there was a very small door on the front of the Olympic gates and after giving them a quick kick we were in! We walked down the Tunnel (or up the tunnel to be precise) in the footsteps of great United Captains, Byrne, Charlton, Robson and of course Bobby Moore in 66. I highly doubt any of those were wearing a Jim Leighton Condom T Shirt. We had a walk on the pitch and then up into the Royal Box, shrugged our shoulders and decided... pub. Five minutes later we were in an empty Green Man!

Back to the League Cup Final and Wednesday simply wanted it more. United fan John Sheridan scored the only goal and the only other incident of note was a nasty injury to Les Sealey. He took a gash to the knee that went right down to the bone and had an almighty row with Jim McGregor on the pitch, refusing to come off (it got more telly time for Jim's Morson International cap).

We went home disappointed but not really that arsed as we were all making Faustian pacts with old Lucifer himself. You can have that one, we don't mind losing… just as long as we can win the Cup Winners Cup! Yes we were in the midst of Euro Fever as we were just one game away from our first European Final since 1968.

Montpellier were first up in the Quarter Final (my first game in the now seated North Stand Lower) and the roof came off OT when Choccy scored in the first minute. Unfortunately Wembley hero Lee Martin stuck one in his own goal and we had a lot to do in the second leg. This was the first real accessible Euro awayer for the Red Army and they travelled in their thousands. Clayton Blackmore was having a fantastic season at Left Back and scored another crucial free kick to put us one up. As reliable as Sunbeds free kicks were Steve Bruce's penalties and he sent the travelling reds into rapture with the crucial Second goal and a new chant was born,

"Always Look on the Bright Side of Life".

To reach the final in Rotterdam we were going to have to beat one of our old enemies Barcelona or Juventus, unless we got lucky and drew Legia Warsaw. No one could believe it when we drew the Poles and even more so when we put in a thoroughly professional 3-1 away win through McClair, Hughes and Bruce. Now everybody was getting very giddy and provisionally booking time off and dusting off the passport. The Home leg was a slightly nervy but regulation 1-1 draw and we were through to the final vs Barcelona and I had a big decision to make.

23. ROTTERDAM*

We had pretty much known we were going to be in the final after that first leg in Warsaw so decisions were made whether we were in or out. My initial thoughts were that I was out. Going to European awayers is what other people did. I couldn't go, could I? At the semi final second leg I picked up a flyer for UF Tours on Warwick Road. £120 (£60 deposit) got you two nights in Rotterdam and a 'guaranteed match ticket' getting there by Boat and Coach. Shay had initially said he was out, Chris was out because he was already booked on a family holiday to Greece (he sent me a postcard to say he had 'collected a blow' which was nice) and Darren was out because he couldn't afford it. Pete however was in (along with Tim and Jock who we went to Highbury 6-2 with) and we decided to go with UF Tours.

Since qualifying there had been a lot of talk about how this was the first time an English Team reached the final since The Heysel Disaster of 85 and all the talk was that United were going to have no alcohol on their trip. We weren't having any of that! We were going to trust someone would give us a ticket and that we wouldn't be in a shithole. I went to the Post Office and got my One Year Passport (I had never been abroad before!) and strutted around like Bexy in *'The Firm'*. Then my Dad had a word in my shell like. He wasn't comfortable with the great unknowns involved and wanted me to go on the United trip instead. £62 including a match ticket and no stopovers. To be honest I was a bit relieved! I rang Pete to tell him the bad news and he thought it was a great idea. I think all their Dad's had the same conversation! We lost our deposits but I think it was the right choice.

Then Shay threw a spanner in the works and said he was going!

He had persuaded his mate to go on the Club Trip but they were going to fly in and out for about double the price. I was pleased for Shay but a little bit gutted at the same time. I wanted to be the one from the family who went! I soon got over my little hissy fit.

As Dad or Danny weren't going then we could have the Season Tickets which put us a lot further up the pecking order. There was one very big problem though, the Season Ticket Holders had to produce their passports when purchasing their ticket. Now as I mentioned before, most of the Season Ticket Holders were actually dead and the talk in the cantilever stand at The Derby was one of panic! How was I going to use the Season Ticket when my Grandad died in 1980! We hatched a plan and I rang the ticket office and put on an old man's voice, coughing and spluttering like Bob Fleming on *The Fast Show*.

"Cough cough, hello it's Mr Taylor here. I'm a bit under the weather so I will be sending my Grandson to buy the ticket, is that ok splutter splutter". The lad on the other end of the phone sounded like he had been fielding these calls all morning.

"Yes Mr Taylor, as long as your 'Grandson' has an up to date passport then he can pick up the ticket". Result, but I had forgotten to ask if the passports would be checked against the season ticket holder at any later point so I had to ring back,

"Cough splutter, hello you don't know me and you definitely didn't just speak to me etc." Clearly United had decided to turn a blind eye but not everybody knew that. I went down to the ticket office on my dinner time walk round the ground and people were queuing up with pretend limps, dressed like old men and looking like Ponsonby from *Blackadder II* with a bag on their head lol.

On the Saturday before the game I collected my Gilders and went into my local Barber Shop and said

"Make me look like Lee Sharpe!". A few hours later, my Brother Shay who is Ten years older than me marched into his local barbers and said

"Make me look like Lee Sharpe!".

We all had our tickets, money and haircuts... next stop Rotterdam*.

*This is, of course, The Wedding Present song 'Rotterdam' and not The Beautiful South version which is coming up... now.

24. ROTTERDAM (OR ANYWHERE)

The coach was to leave Old Trafford at 10pm on Tuesday Night to head down for the Dover-Calais Ferry. We therefore got to The Dog and Partridge at about 6 for what would possibly be our last drinks of the trip. The Dog was a riot with all the songs and nervous energy ahead of our mammoth journey. Everyone drank as much as they could and preyed that the coach had a toilet (it did).

On walking round to OT we were greeted with a momentous sight with dozens of coaches loading up. BBC North West News were there conducting interviews and it felt like we were marching off to war! I hoped to get a couple of hours of shut eye on the way down but was too excited/needed the toilet. Certain parts of the trip are still crystal clear in my mind. BBC Radio Solent was playing on the coach and the featured artist was early 80's New Romantics, Modern Romance. About 3am and a coach full of loved up Mancs singing

"Ay Ay Ay Ay Moosey and Best Years of our Lives!"

We had to hang around in the car park before embarking and someone had brought a football. A big game of headers and volleys ensued and yes, I did try and execute an overhead kick. I'm lucky I didn't end up in Folkestone General! This feeling could not be beaten and I kept having to stop to take it all in. To the sounds of the hum of the port, under a clear night sky and with some very suspicious 'weed' smells, we were playing football and going to see United in a European Final and I wasn't yet 19 years old. The sights, the sounds, the smells will never leave me.

Boarding the boat everyone made for the Bar and it was open! I mistakenly asked for Bitter (forgetting I was in the South) and got served it in a bottle with one of those funny Grolsch tops. Who cares, I had another Beer in my hand and was living the dream. We disembarked at Calais and it was my first time on foreign soil. No more Modern Romance but maybe we will be treated to some Serge Gainsbourg, Edith Piaf, Vanessa Paradis or some early Daft Punk. The first song we heard was *'The One and Only'* by Chesney Hawkes. Ah well, we sang anyway. Being the gregarious funny fucker that I am, I seemed to be keeping everyone entertained on the coach although I think second hand smoke from the sheer amount of spliffs helped lol. We stopped at a service station in Antwerp where a few people necked cans, got a strip wash in the loo and grabbed a bite to eat. I just stared in awe at the sheer amount of porno mags on sale. And they were at eye level too (yes I know we were in Belgium but I had been whistling the *'Van der Valk'* theme tune since the semi finals!). As we approached Rotterdam I remember us pulling onto a motorway and alongside a coach of Dutch Pensioners (what a band they were). They all waved nervously at us and I gleaned from their expressions that they were worried we were all hooligans. I hadn't even considered there might be mither but it wasn't something I got involved in.

We finally got off the coach at about noon local time and it was raining a lot. Thankfully there was a low roofed bar with a covered terrace outside called De Ballentent and we got in there with our gilders in hand! What followed was 5 hours of bliss.

"Drink drink wherever you may be, we are the drunk and disorderly
And we don't give a shit and we don't give a fuck
We're coming home with the Cup Winners Cup!"

We sheltered from the rain and sang our hearts out. I did not see one Barcelona supporter and the reds really were everywhere. During a lull in the weather we had a wander to a big park nearby where there was a stage set up and Manchester Band The High were on stage. Reds swapped hats with Dutch police who were doing the conga to *'Box Set Go'*. I hadn't eaten since Manchester so got myself a Cheeseburger. This is very important to the story. The coach was due to leave to go to the Stadium at 5.30pm and I put my head against the coach window and closed my eyes. I was then very aware of the sensation of throwing up but that was ok because it was just a bad dream. Hang on, the vomit isn't stopping and here comes the Cheese Burger! I couldn't believe it. Clearly it was the Cheeseburger and not the hours of drinking that did for me, "Ahem.'" I didn't feel ill, just embarrassment and the realisation that not just was I covered in sick but the coach was going to smell of sick all the way home. I'm surprised I wasn't lynched. There was a very real conversation that I would be kicked off the coach but thankfully some of the lads who we were talking to stuck up for me. I reckon Pete, Tim and Jock probably wanted me thrown off lol. I was glad I was wearing my Wax Jacket as it absorbed the river of Amstelpuke quite well and I could clean it off quickly. What I really needed was that bloke from Norwich who knew all about dry cleaning. I ate a couple of my Digestives (the only food I brought with me!) to take away the taste and composed myself, the stadium was in site.

25. IF I HADN'T SEEN SUCH RICHES

We arrived at the stadium and fuck me, the Dutch Riot Police look scary. We posed for some pictures and made our way up to the top tier, behind the goal. They were bucket type seats and each seat was filled with about three inches of water. One of the lads had a Union Flag which, came in very handy to try and clear the water but there was no escaping a very cold wet arse when you sat down. We were ridiculously early for an 8.15 pm kick off but at least it helped sober me up a bit and the rain was helping clean my coat.

It was pretty obvious that the majority of the stadium was filled with United fans but at the other end of the ground I saw the Barca fans for the first time. A familiar voice could be heard on the tannoy, it was Keith 'Kid' Fane who had taken over from Tom Tyrrell as pre-match host at Old Trafford. One of his innovations was Stretford End Karaoke where he tried to get people to sing along to a popular track before the game and most people would sing the first line of Mustang Sally and then shout 'You Scouse Bastards' or similar, much to the amusement of The Stretford End. He did find one diamond in the rough though, a teenage girl called Tracey Malone who sang *'I'm So Excited'* by The Pointer Sisters. It went down very well and the following week she was invited onto the pitch to sing it in front of The Stretford End. I'm not gonna lie, I don't know if it was the big coat, the hooped earrings or the scraped back hair but Tracey was right up my street and I nipped to the loos at the back of the Stretford Paddock to crack one off. We did say this was a warts and all book right? Tracey even got to appear on *The Hitman and Her* with a new version of her anthem called *'I'm so Excited, its Man United'*.

"We've got Webby, Incey, Les Sealey he's the best
You know it's Clayton, Sparky, Mark Robins and the rest.

And when we score a goal, we lose control!"

I certainly lost control, Trace. What's funny is that I recognise her through Facebook and often see her walking her Dog near my house!

So back at De Kuip and sadly Tracey wasn't being rolled out to sing but we did have the first airing of the night of *'Always Look on the Bright Side of Life'*. The marker had been put down to El Keitho Fanio to play something for the Barcelona fans to sing in response. The now familiar opening bars of the Barca anthem 'Cant del Barca' rang out and the supporters came to life;

"Tot el camp (clap clap clap)
Es un clam (clap clap clap)
Tot el camp
és un clam
som la gent blau-grana.
Tant se val d'on venim
si del sud o del nord
ara estem d'acord, estem d'acord,
una bandera ens agermana.
Blau-grana al vent
un crit valent
tenim un nom
el sap tothom:

Barça, Barça, Barça!"

They had flags going and fireworks and it was very impressive. How were we going to top that as the only other song he had in his arsenal was *Glory Glory Man United*? *'Come on United, let's sing it for Manchester'* shouted Fane like a drunk uncle at a wedding and the opening strains of *'Sit Down'* by James could be heard and my heart sank. Yeah it's a good chorus but not everybody knows it. It was then that something quite glorious happened. A moment that still brings goosebumps and grown men to tears. 30,000 United fans began to sing;

> *"I'll sing myself to sleep,*
> *A song from the darkest hour.*
> *Secrets I can't keep*
> *Inside of a day..."*

On that freezing cold wet night as dusk approached, fuelled by Oranjeboom and (some) with vomit on their Wax Jackets, they sang the whole song, verses and chorus, word for word and it was beautiful

> *"...Now I've swung back down again*
> *It's worse than it was before*
> *If I hadn't seen such*
> *I could live with being poor.*
> **Oh Sit Down**
> **Oh Sit Down**
> **Oh Sit Down**
> **Sit Down next to me**
> *Sit Down (sit down, sit down, sit down, down)*
> *In sympathy."*

It was a song of hope, of putting your arm around the person stood next to you, of holding on to a piece of home and it sounded fucking epic! We roared as the song finished and the Catalans accepted defeat and all stood to an hombre and applauded back. If you speak to anyone, *anyone* who went to Rotterdam they will all stare into the middle distance and say, '*Sit Down*'. It was our Vietnam moment!

26.   UNBELIEVABLE

Our biggest fear was of course a good pasting. We took some comfort that Barcelona were without two key players. Goalkeeper Andoni Zubizarreta and the brilliant Bulgarian striker Hristo Stoichkov. They were replaced by Carles Busquets and some lump called Julio Salinas. Busquets wore trackie bottoms (tracksuit pants). All goalies who wear trackie bottoms are shit. Speaking of keepers, United only had one injury worry and that was Les Sealey who still hadn't played since his horror injury in the League Cup Final. It's often said (including by the great man himself) that Fergie is a lucky manager. Well he certainly got lucky with the decision to play Sealey as he was nowhere near fit. I genuinely think that if Gary Walsh hadn't had such a poor game on the Saturday before at Crystal Palace then he might have got the nod.

Finally the kick off arrived and as the teams took to the pitch the fireworks started in the Barca end. That and the persistent rain made for very poor visibility and from my lofty perch it looked like United were wearing plain white T Shirts. Of course when I eventually saw the one off kit we wore for the final, I totally fell in love with it! It's still one of my favourite kits ever.

Barca began by knocking the ball around and generally looking very good whereas United looked nervous, especially Lee Sharpe. Maybe he was bogged down by the expectations of all those haircuts. Finally United created a big chance from an unlikely source. Gary Pallister played a wonderful defence splitting pass through to Brian McClair. Choccy had scored in every round so far and bore down on goal before skying it into the United fans behind the goal. It was a massive chance and would they regret it?

Shay of course had gone with one of his workmates by plane and arrived about an hour before kick off. He hadn't had a drink yet so queued at the bar. He got to the front and spoke very slowly and very loud to the barman.

"T-w-o, t-w-o, pints of l-a-g-e-r, you know l-a-g-e-r"

"Yeah alright mate, keep yer hair on". He was from Wythenshawe.

We had also agreed that whatever the score, at Half Time we would both stand on our seats and wave to try and find each other. How hard could it be? I waved furiously and spotted him straight away! We managed to convey through the medium of mime that we were both ok, had a good view and we were still in the game. I wondered if I would ever get the chance to actually sit with him at a European Final?

United came out for the Second Half on the front foot and created half chances. Hughes fashioned a chance very similar to the one in which he scored in the semi final in Warsaw but it was deflected wide and Lee Sharpe hooked one just off target after Busquets had been caught out of position, probably looking for the nearest Sports Direct for some more trackies.

Finally in the 67th minute, the breakthrough came. Hughes had won a free kick after yet another battle with swarthy centre half Nando. Robson floated a ball in that half tempted Busquets out of his goal but landed straight on the head of Steve Bruce who guided it into the far corner for his 20th goal of the season. Or at least it was that right until Mark Hughes tapped it in as it was crossing the line. It wasn't until the next day that I realised Hughes had scored. A lot of the focus was on Hughes of course. He had failed miserably when he signed for Barcelona in 1986 so he had a lot to prove and boy did he prove it seven minutes later.

Robson was again the creator putting the Welshman through on goal. Once again Busquets came flying out only this time Hughes hurdled over him but has surely taken it far too wide? Not for Sparky. This was the man who wasn't a great goal scorer but a scorer of great goals and this was one of the best, as he twatted it first time past the retreating defenders to put the reds 2-0 in front. We went absolutely mental as surely that was game over.

This seemed to wake Barca who suddenly started moving the ball around quickly and Laudrup was becoming more and more influential. He forced a foul out of Robson about 30 yards from goal which was a dangerous position with Ronald Koeman about. The Dutchman had a fantastic record from free kicks and just 5 minutes after falling 2-0 behind, he fired in a free kick, Sealey went down in instalments and Barca were back in the game at 2-1.

There were now just 10 minutes left and United had totally run out of steam. Defending in numbers and inviting the Catalans on. Hughes still played on the break and tried to force his way through for an attempt at a Hat Trick only to be hauled down by Nando which earned him a red card (if you turned it over there was a green card underneath. Nando? Oh never mind).

Time was now really running out and I can still remember vividly seeing the look on Steve Bruce's face as his attempted pass back to Sealey was never going to make it. Substitute Pinilla intercepted and danced round the stricken keeper not once but twice before laying it back to Michael Laudrup who stabbed it towards the empty net. 30,000 collective United hearts were in their throats until Clayton Blackmore who had scored our very first goal of the campaign appeared on the line to clear it away. It was cheered as loud as any goal and that was it! We were coming home with the Cup Winners Cup!

The celebrations at the end were memorable. We sang *'Always Look on the Bright Side of Life'* into the night with Ferguson conducting the singing. Our first European trophy since 1968 and the first on foreign soil. Oh yeah, we have a massive journey home on a coach that smells of sick! I got back on the coach and put my head on the window. I kid you not, I opened my eyes and we were driving onto the ferry at Calais. I slept the entire way home including a half hour stop in Antwerp again!

When I got home on Thursday morning, my Dad had lined up all the papers on the dining room table for me. He went to give me a hug for getting home safely and then stopped at the smell.

"Oh someone threw up on me on the ferry" I said.

"Of course they did son, of course they did".

27.   TURNED UP, CLOCKED ON, LAID OFF

I loved my job. Always did. A bit like following your Football team, you don't particularly like the club but you love the shirt and the people you go with. I found work the same. You never always agreed with what the board did, false promises on bonuses, redundancies, the Spicy Sandwich Lady etc. but I always liked the people I worked with. Of course there were some utter fucking Thundercunts who worked there but also some people who became friends for life. I'm still in a message group with friends from work, the mysteriously named *'Pelt, Bantz and Brendan'*.

I worked for a Plant Hire company called M&H Plant Hire. They were founded in Weaste in the early 70's before relocating to the glamour of Trafford House in 1973. For those that don't know, that's the big multi storey building on Chester Road that you would see on Sky Sports News when they were interviewing people on the forecourt. Working next to Old Trafford definitely had its advantages. I remember sending Darren to the Ticket Office for 92 League Cup Final Tickets and I could see from the window which ones he got. Wave your arms for Upper Tier and point down for Lower Tier. Kind of an early version of the Kolo Toure dance. I also used to go to The Dog and Partridge at dinner. If you thought it was a shithole on Match Days then you should have seen it on a wet Monday Afternoon in February. However building up a rapport with Mad Anne behind the bar meant that on Match Days she would always serve me first and not charge Match Day prices.

As I had said earlier, my original plan was to just stay at M&H until I could find something else within the Newspaper industry and in the meantime I would use my wages on Wine, Women and The Wedding Present. The problem was that I went to more games that season than any before or since. 48 games that season compared to 40 the season before and 42 the season after. 55 of these games were awayers so as you can imagine I was always staying another month because there were more games coming up etc. etc. etc. (I've just remembered the Yul Brynner like image on the side of Tommy's Fireplaces at Trafford Bar, that'll separate the match going reds from the muggles. I digress).

M&H was spread over two floors. The 9th Floor is where the bourgeoisie worked. The Directors, board room and oddly the canteen. Gin soaked old dodderers who pinched the arses and sometimes more of the predominantly female staff. I worked on the 10th Floor where there were only 3 male members of staff. 2 of those were Managers so just one bloke was on the same level as me. His name was John and we are still best friends today. It was only after we both got promoted (the women loved that) and I got his job that we became friendly. I discovered he was a Red and we had similar tastes in music. We both loved The Smiths and Gary Numan and introduced each other to our other favourites.

Being a gregarious so and so, I had no problem working with so many women. When I started I was a slender 18 year old with a Barney Sumner hair do and I could feel the women mentally undressing me. As I got older and stayed there longer I could feel them mentally putting them back on again. We got paid weekly and every Friday we would go to Stretford Arndale to draw out our money and get a McDonalds. One such afternoon just before Christmas, a girl called Pam was driving and we pulled out of Moss Lane to cross Derbyshire Lane and down Victoria Road to park up when we suddenly shunted up the arse and not in a good way. We were thrown forward into a wall and then rolled backwards into the road. I closed my eyes and awaited death.

Something was bound to plough into us and I'm hoping it's not a 257 bus. Thankfully everything had stopped when they saw the crash. We all checked we were ok and there was an Ambulance already there.

"Bloody hell, you were quick" I said.

"Quick? We were the ones who hit you!'

It turns out that they were on a shout and were driving on the wrong side of the road with no sirens on. Thankfully there was a witness who saw everything but it was still nerve wracking going up in court against Ambulance drivers! I 'only' had whiplash thank goodness although it did mean I had to go and see The Fall the next night at Stockport Town Hall wearing a neck brace.

Considering what a good mate John was we actually only went to one United game together. 2-2 draw vs Sunderland in the 96 FA Cup Run. He had a season ticket and for years we would meet up in or outside The Dog and Partridge and then the Blaize but only went to one match. Well actually that's not strictly true because I persuaded him that we should get tickets for the Euro 96 Semi Final at OT. It cost £55 a ticket which is a lot of money now, never mind over 25 years ago but it would definitely be worth it as we are guaranteed two top teams and an incredible atmosphere. As it is we got France vs Czech Republic and the ground was only half full. We were sitting in J Stand but right next to some French fans in The North Stand. We had put a few away in The Robin Hood beforehand so when the French National Anthem, *La Marseillaise*, began to play we sang along with gusto,

"*Ooh Aah Cantona!*" etc.

As it finished I leant over to a French fan waving a flag next to me to wish him

"*Bonne Chance?*" His retort was

"FUCK OFF! FUCK OFF!" So much for *Entente Cordiale*!

What followed was by far, the worst game of Football I have ever had the misfortune to attend. We went down at Half Time to get a pint and didn't actually return until about the 60 minute mark. At 90 minutes, people streamed out of the stadium in droves, not just because it was terrible but to get home in time for the England vs Germany Semi Final at Wembley. Even if I left now I was unlikely to get back to New Moston, where I lived, in time for kick off. Thankfully John lived in Stretford and invited me to watch it there. It did however mean I had to sit through Extra Time. At one point in the Second Half of Extra Time John hadn't even noticed that they had changed ends and thought a French player was clean through when it was actually a defender. Full Time was 0-0 and both sides were lucky to get nil. By the time the penalties came we were openly heckling the players and ready to kick off with the mouthy frog next to us.

We have been best mates in good times and bad. Whether it was our daily walk around the stadium or on the piss in Wigan with our mate Rob, we were there for each other. I actually got locked in the toilets of Stilettos Lap Dancing Bar in Wigan, just as there was a power cut! I rang him to rescue me and he felt his way in the dark (a perilous task given our surroundings) and then he came and kicked the door down for me. John had a season ticket in K Stand for the 96-97 Season and let me have his seat on December 21st as his wife was in labour and his Daughter Amy was born the next day. It turned out to be the 5-0 win containing 'that' Eric chip and every time they show that goal, which is quite often, I would smile and think of Amy who was also my God Daughter. In January 2020, Amy passed away most unexpectedly and it was every bit as heartbreaking as you can imagine. Every time I see that Eric goal now I still think of Amy but it is filled with sorrow.

John was made redundant in 2002. I wasn't really in a position to leave in protest like Rob did but it was a very difficult time. Redundancy regularly swung over Hewden (previously M&H) like The Sword of Damocles. I first got made redundant in 2008 and then again in 2015 but I always managed to find another role. I would like to think it was because my work ethic was appreciated and not because I ran the Company Quiz Night. Redundancy caught up with me again in 2016 only this time I took it voluntarily. In 2014 I had been diagnosed with a condition called Cluster Headaches (my mate Nige reckons he saw them supporting Bauhaus at Leeds Duchess of York in 1982. Funny fucker that he is). They are the worst pain a human can suffer and have ruined my life over the last 8 years since diagnosis. That however may be for another book.

What I do know is that I could no longer cope with work and the Cluster Headaches so when I was invited to reapply for positions in my Department I decided it was time to take Voluntary Redundancy, even though it was made clear to me that they wanted me to stay. That Quiz night wasn't going to write itself.

28.   IN YOUR FACE

After reaching three cup finals in two years, United had the taste of success and now it was time to go for the big one, The First Division Title. It had been 24 long years since the last success and there was a definite feeling that Liverpool were on the wane after Dalglish's implosion the year before. Fergie brought in two new signings but in reality it felt like four. Andrei Kanchelskis had been signed towards the end of the previous season and played in the defeat to Crystal Palace in the last league match of the season. What I had seen of him in the reserves, was that he was rapid! Another player who put in a couple of appearances but was then going to be a regular member of the squad was Ryan Giggs. He had been spoken about as the next big thing for a while and may have been bloodied earlier but for the superb form of Lee Sharpe.

The two new signings were Paul Parker from QPR and Peter Schmeichel from Brondby. They didn't get off to the best start with a defensive mix up in Sir Matt Busby's Testimonial vs Republic of Ireland but as I took my seat in B Stand for the opening game vs Notts County, hopes amongst the shirt sleeved crowd were high. A comfortable 2-0 win followed with a worldie from Robbo, but it was Kanchelskis who caught the eye with a magnificent home debut. I'm talking up there with the debuts of Ronaldo, Rooney, Macheda and Martial, he was that good. Bring on Aston Villa!

There was a first for our away travels as we went by Car. Pete had a Ford Escort (I think, I know nothing about cars) and offered to drive. Darren and Tim made up the numbers and we met by the Petrol Station near The Old Cock to fuel up. I knew Pete had a tape deck so I bought along two bangers on cassette. Seamonsters by The Wedding Present and ex:el by 808 State.

All was going well and we were looking forward to hopefully getting there in time for a pint and seeing Andrei again. Then as we started to approach Birmingham the car started to really splutter. Luckily Hilton Park Services was in sight but we had to push it the final 100 yards along the hard shoulder. An RAC man was there under his 'brolly and asked did we need any help?

"Oh yes please" we answered to which he replied there was an £80 joining fee. So that was a no then!

We soon realised the problem. The petrol cap was missing. Pete swore it was there when he put the petrol in but cannot promise that he didn't put the cap on top of the car. We gave it time to cool down and shoved a rag into the hole and hoped for the best. There was a mixture of apprehension and gallows humour as we inched up the M6 to the lovelorn Albini influenced grunge of The Wedding Present and the electronic beeps of 808 State (or Bob State as Guy Meyler, the writer of the Manchester Evening News Diary section once called them). We crawled past The RAC Building and approached the big flyover bridge. The Traffic was slow because of the match and one lane on the bridge being out. Then disaster struck as the car completely conked out. No amount of trying the engine was going to work, we were stuck and now totally blocking the way. We had to get the car into the lane that was closed down by pushing it right across the oncoming traffic! We had played with the big boys and thought we could drive there but now felt very much like schoolboys as abuse rained down on us from the other cars.

We eventually got the car into the spare lane and could see Villa Park but we were on foot by the busiest junction in Europe! Then a passing car with a couple of Reds driving popped a window and shouted "I've got room for Two". Me and Darren threw each other a glance like Eastwood and Van Cleef, the complex and experimental yet melodic beats of the State were replaced by whip cracks and coyote howls straight from the Morricone playbook. Without thinking the pair of us dived into the car without so much as a look back and left Tim, Pete and his stricken motor. Now we were laughing of course but still had the small problem of how we would get home? We went straight to the ground and in amongst the bucket hats and middle partings of the Madchester heavy reds, I spotted the unmistakable moustache of Uncle Danny a few rows away (I think he would have been harder to spot on Canal Street). Even better, a Steve Bruce penalty made it two wins out of two for the reds.

I rang Pete the next day (no mobile phones!) very much with my tail between my legs. He totally understood though and said they probably would have done the same thing! He stayed with the car whilst Tim hitched to the ground, stopping to ring Pete's Dad with the bad news. He came to collect him just as the final whistle was sounding. There were no hard feelings though but he made one thing clear.

"You aren't getting those two tapes back". Fair enough.

The reds rolled onto Goodison Park on the Saturday and this time it was me and Chris playing it safe on the coach. There was some disappointment that Kanchelskis had been called up by Russia/CIS so was missing. Whenever we travelled to Goodison and Anfield we would laugh at the sheer amount of Shell Suits that the Scousers were wearing, doing nothing to veer away from the supposed stereotyping of Harry Enfield.

"Are we playing count the shell suits today?" I ask Chris to which someone on the seat in front leans back and in all seriousness says

"Nah he's away on International Duty this weekend!" Brilliant.

Big Pete proved that he was more than just someone who could throw the ball a long way with an inspired performance as we sneaked a goalless draw. 7 points out of 9, the title charge was on.

29. THE 90'S REVIVAL

The season was going very well and United were playing some of their best football in years. In Schmeichel they had a potent attacking weapon with that incredible throw (some would say he was a weapon of a different kind but that's just opinion). His throws to release Giggs and Kanchelskis changed English Football. That isn't over exaggerating, the likes of his throw had never been seen before. Suddenly keepers up and down the land (and I include playing 5 a Side down the Pitz, JJB Soccer Dome or George Carnell Sports Centre) were suddenly looking to throw the ball out overarm as soon as they received it.

Against Oldham Athletic in the League Cup they got a standing ovation off the pitch at Half Time. They were that good. I went to most matches that season either in The Stretford End or Stretford Paddock. We had discovered a little known turnstile for the Paddock which was for Under 16's and only £2.50. I was 19 at this stage and would often turn up with a hangover and five o clock shadow but I never got pulled.

We surrendered our Cup Winners Cup title against a much better Atletico Madrid side (ah well, we'll always have Rotterdam) but the unbeaten run in the league lasted into October. Darren was now living in Sheffield as he went to 'Poly' there and he invited me and Chris for the weekend where we played Sheffield Wednesday. The reds were 2-1 up when Wednesday brought Nigel Jemson on.

"He's nothing to worry about" I assured the boys. Two Jemson goals later and United's unbeaten run was over. Still it was Chris's birthday so we planned to get bladdered. Darren's flatmates were both away for the weekend so we decided to wear their clothes and after shave for the night out!

What became apparent was our main rivals would be another Yorkshire side, Leeds United. Only promoted the season before they had a good season and those two titanic battles vs United in the League Cup Semi Final. They were now turning sides over including a 6-1 demolition of Sheffield Wednesday in front of the Live TV Cameras.

Still United were going well and one great away win I went to was at Crystal Palace. I was very hungover from the night before as I had gone in The Nelson in Urmston for a few Joey Holts with Paul. Why was I going to the pub with someone I actively tried to avoid? The ramifications of saying no were too great and a lot of the time he was ok company. He was a big red of course and his taste in music wasn't too shabby. Ultravox, Talking Heads and Erasure were all good and I had gotten him into The Stone Roses and New Order. In fact when he moved into a flat in Chorlton with his girlfriend he was next door neighbours with Mani when they were in their pomp. He used to smoke weed with him and Ian Brown and said neither of them had a pot to piss in! Anyhow back to The Nelson and Paul has got talking to some randomer and asking him his favourite subject

"If something happened to me would you care?" Proper full on philosophical bollocks and this other guy was stoned enough to join in. Just as I was ready to leave he told me we had been invited to a House Party in Partington. I told him no because I had to go to London the next day and for fuck sake Paul, Partington! Even the buses stopped running there after 7pm. Still he told me we were going and who did I think I was to say no? I had changed apparently and thought I was better than everyone. He then punched me to be sure I understood.

Fast forward a few hours and I'm bored out of my tree at this party. I was the only one not smoking weed and it had got to the stage of the night when Pink Fucking Floyd were playing. Some bloke sidles up next to me and says

"Ahh, I love Pink Floyd. Bat out of Hell is brilliant". It took every ounce of resistance not to burst out laughing. Why did I not do weed? Well I didn't smoke for starters and I saw what it did to Paul and how it can lead onto harder drugs. Just not for me. Even today when everybody tells me the odd medicinal doobie will be good for pain relief in relation to my Cluster Headaches but I just can't do it.

Just a few hours later I'm waiting outside The Dog and Partridge for the Red Issue Coach. Chris looks equally rough after a night fingering in The Bamboo, Hazel Grove (probably). Then the worst thing happens. The Coach pulls up on the other side of Chester Road. We could have run down to the main lights and crossed there but everyone went in a straight line and were going to hurdle the barriers in the middle of the road. Me and Chris both cock our leg over and it's a monumental effort to get over and that's when Chris utters the immortal words "Tits and Hangovers" to describe our efforts. For some reason it makes us laugh all the way to London and even to this day, if faced with a particularly difficult hurdle, be it physical or metaphorical, I will say Tits and Hangovers.

I had only been to Selhurst Park once before, a timid 2-0 defeat to Charlton Athletic two years before. Now we looked like a team ready to storm the league. Giggs was unplayable in a 3-1 victory and we really dared to dream. In our way stood Leeds United. The game vs Leeds at Elland Road was looming and looked massive even though it was 4 months before the season ended. For some inexplicable reason Donald Trump had conducted the draw for the Quarter Final of the Rumbelows Cup and pulled out us going to Leeds in a rematch of the previous season. That night the draw for the 3rd Round of the FA Cup was being done on Match of the Day, late on the Saturday night. We came out of Corkers (Urmston's one and only Nightclub) and into the chippy for a kebab. We asked who United had got in the cup draw.

"Leeds Away, Boss" he answered.

"No the FA Cup draw?"

"Yep, Leeds Away." We had been drawn to play each other 3 times in 11 days, all at Elland Road!

I was successful in getting tickets for 2 out of the 3 games, only missing out on the FA Cup game. For reasons I can't remember I had tickets for both games on my own. The others were either unsuccessful or skint from Christmas but my trip to Elland Road for the League game was my first awayer on my own. As it happens it was pretty uneventful and finished in a 1-1 draw. Next up was the FA Cup and the game was postponed on the day of the game due to a waterlogged pitch. I had also picked up a terrible cold meaning I couldn't go to the Rumbelows Cup game. I watched it at a mates house and was left speechless by a brilliant 3-1 win and also because I literally couldn't speak as I had lost my voice. We also won the rearranged FA Cup game meaning we had knocked them out of both Cup competitions. This of course felt wonderful but with hindsight was the worst thing that happened to us. That and the arrival of a feisty Frenchman.

30.   JE SUIS UN ROCK STAR

I'd never heard of Eric Cantona. When the story broke that the 'enfant terrible' of French Football was having a trial at Sheffield Wednesday. It didn't really register on the importance scale. I looked a bit more interested when I heard Howard Wilkinson had snapped him up for Leeds. Although the title was billed as *'The War of the Roses'*, neither side was playing particularly well. United had started 1992 with an embarrassing 4-1 defeat at home to Queens Park Rangers. In fact from that point until the end of the season, we didn't win two league games in a row for the rest of the campaign. Leeds weren't much better but the difference is that they had bought in a new face to freshen things up. *'Vive la Difference'*.

However before The King's arrival in Yorkshire, I had an appointment on enemy territory myself. Barrie and I wanted to see Half Man Half Biscuit in Leeds. It was however the night before I was going to see United at Arsenal the next day. Just thinking about it now gives me the heebee-geebees but at the time it sounded like a weekender (a great Flowered Up song, I should have saved that for a chapter title). It was a Foggy late January night when we hopped on the National Express to that Leeds. The third part of the United vs Leeds trilogy had been just a fortnight before and I was still basking in that glory.

We made our way towards Leeds Uni and it really was a pea-souper of a night. We took a shortcut through a park and suddenly got the distinct feeling we were being followed. We felt like we suddenly couldn't have looked more like Mancs if we had United and City shirts on and walking with Ten to Two Feet shouting 'who is and who isn't!'. I think I have got to know the demographics of the band and these two brothers were not coming to see Half Man Half Biscuit that's for sure.

"Go with me" I whispered to Barrie and then shoved him shouting

"What did you fucking say?" Our would-be attackers looked taken aback but not as much as Baz did!

"Shove me" I said again through gritted teeth and this time Baz realised what my game was.

"Say that again you fucking northern ponce" he screamed and even in a heart thumping moment, Baz was the funniest person in the world and it was a wonder I didn't burst out laughing! It had the desired effect and they did an about turn and retreated.

We had a very drunken night and a brilliant gig but the coach home wasn't until 2.30 am. It had a half hour stopover at Hartshead Moor and still didn't get back to Chorlton Street until 4.30am. Yes we were only coming from Leeds! I then had to wait an hour in Piccadilly Gardens for the first bus of the day home. Quick shower and before you knew it I was on a Red Issue coach with an appointment with The Drayton Park public house near Highbury! We had been thrown out of this pub last time I was here but no such worries this time. The adrenaline kicked in and we sang our hearts out for the lads. These days it's an effort to set the Sky Plus to record the reds when we are on at home, never mind the travelling that we used to do.

A 1-1 draw at Highbury was typical of the results we were getting. As I say Leeds weren't doing much better but Cantona was giving them something different. The revisionists who try to rewrite History will tell you that Cantona only scored three goals in that title run in and that most of his appearances came from the bench, but he gave Leeds a swagger that we were sadly lacking. A lack of ideas and a pudding of a pitch were severely hampering United and victories were few and far between.

Our Quarter Final Rumbelows Cup defeat of Leeds gave us a two legged semi final vs Middlesbrough. The away leg passed without incident (the only thing of note was that I got a lift back off renowned journalist and creator of the United We Stand fanzine, Andy Mitten) but the home game is one of my favourite ever games at Old Trafford and the last great night of The Stretford End! Under the floodlights the game was on a knife edge at 1-1. Lee Sharpe in for the suspended Mark Hughes gave United the lead before Bernie Slaven equalised in front of the massive Boro' following. Whenever any smaller club comes to OT in a cup competition. It always amazes me that people are surprised that they out-sing United. I would expect it every time, be it Aston Villa or Zalaegerszeg. It's their cup final and they are always more up for it. On this night, the Boro' fans were in great voice, we were struggling and the game was heading into Extra Time which, given our run in, we could do without. Our fans understood this and the chanting began, quietly at first before building into an incredible crescendo;

> *"Ferguson's Red and White Army."*
> *"Ferguson's Red and White Army."*
> *"FERGUSON'S RED AND WHITE ARMY!"*

The noise was deafening and the Middlesbrough fans watched on in stunned silence. With Penalties on the horizon, it was a major effort from Neil Webb to get a cross up and off the ground, into the area. The indefatigable Robson steamrollered a header and the ball looped up and onto the waiting foot of Ryan Giggs who sliced a volley into the top corner. This sent the Stretford End into rapture. We were in the Rumbelows Cup Final and then it was the title run in. Surely this was going to be a year to remember?

31. WEEKENDER (AH, THERE IT IS)

I would love to come on here and regale you with tales of legendary rumbles with opposition supporters, main actors, under 5's, stripings and people generally having it on their toes but like most Hooligan books, that would be a work of fiction. We did see the odd bit of mither but we never actively looked for it. This doesn't mean that we didn't enjoy our away trips because we really did. There is something just so much different about an awayer. You do walk with a bounce in your step and stand up and stretch your arms when someone shoots wide. Grade A weapon material!

We occasionally went on the train (for the Arsenal semi final at Villa Park in 2004, I had 4 cans of Stella thinking that should last me to Birmingham. At Crewe, I was banging on the door of the buffet cart for more! And this was 8 in the morning!). Usually though we went by coach, either the official United coach or the Red Issue coach which tended to go a couple of hours earlier to get to the pub.

Before we reach the run in, here are the highlights of 4 awayers after Christmas:

Notts County. Nothing brings out a big away following more than a ground you haven't been to before. It had been 9 years since our last visit to Meadow Lane where thousands of reds partied as news of Raddy Antic's winner at Maine Road drifted in. This game was also pay on the gate so literally thousands of reds turned up without tickets, including us. A mate of ours called Rick went straight to the pub and said the rallying call went out,

"They are shutting the gates" and the pub deserted. We took one look at the scrum to get in and decided to try our luck in the Notts County end. I say end, as their 'popular terrace' actually ran along the side of the pitch, a bit like The Kippax did at City.

We certainly weren't the only ones trying this trick and there were plenty of Reds wearing colours trying to get in. The guy in front of me literally had a big United scarf on, in fact he may have had a butcher's coat covered in Doc's Red Army badges, he was clearly a Red. I was wearing a denim shirt (it was 1992!) with my Rotterdam shirt underneath so it was just poking out.

"Home supporters only, Duck" he probably said. I couldn't believe it as Angus Deayton, Zoe Ball and Mick Hucknall drifted through the turnstile behind me. Thankfully we could glide straight to the turnstile next to us rather than to the back of the queue and this time we got in. I've watched United in the Home End at Celtic and Rangers but never got as much stick as at Notts Fucking County.

The Reds were poor and Clayton Blackmore salvaged a 1-1 draw with a late penalty. Once back in Manchester, me and Darren, to use his Sunday name, went to a flat warming party that Paul was throwing. He had moved into a flat in Salford with his girlfriend which obviously I was very pleased about. We were both uncertain whether to go or not as Darren had been bullied by Paul too. Not physically but racist abuse. It wasn't that he didn't like my best mate, far from it but as kids he used to call him names. Whenever we would play at the front he would say that Darren was a Russian Footballer called "Niggerlov" and that he used to eat Coon Flakes for Breakfast. All very childish stuff and all very hurtful. At the height of the George Floyd scandal recently I messaged Darren and apologised for never standing up to Paul when he called him these names. He said there was no need for me to apologise and understood the pressure I was under. Another time we were playing Snooker in my bedroom and Paul insisted on potting the balls with his Dick whilst singing

"That's the way aha aha I like it". Rather like me, I doubt that Darren can ever hear that song the same again.

Still the lure of a few cans was the winner and we went to the party. We were heavily into Vic Reeves at the time and we spoke in a language Paul didn't understand. We were both in top form, maybe exaggerating our exploits in the Notts County end but all in all, we were young men and not little boys to be bullied anymore. When the party was over, we sat and watched a video of Thomas Hearns knockouts and as I drifted off to sleep, I received a classic Hearns jab right in my mush. I pretended to still be asleep. He just couldn't resist letting me know who was boss.

Southampton. This was an FA Cup game played on a Monday Night on BSkyB. Me and Chris boarded the double decker coach for the long journey down South. It was a freezing cold night and when we arrived we set off in search of a pub. We both tied our scarves around our faces and set off. We then realised that we probably looked like 'Napoli Youth' and weren't to be messed with! Another dire draw followed, 0-0 this time and it was the early hours when we got back to OT. Chris had recently passed his driving test and had promised to drive me back to Urmston. Freezing fog had set in and we drove down Stretford Road with me telling him where the bends in the road were as you literally couldn't see your hand in front of your face!

Sheffield United. This time we were on the train as we were going to stay at Darren's student digs as we had earlier that season for the Sheffield Wednesday game. We were putting away the pints of Wards and were pretty pissed come kick off. Sheff U were 1-0 up at Half Time and it looked like our wretched run on the road was going to continue when first Brian McClair and then Clayton Blackmore scored late goals to secure three precious points and more excitedly not destroy our weekender!

We had a hilarious night although there was a near miss in The

Howard, the big Blades pub near the Train Station. Just as I was about to order, someone shouted that

"We've just slashed a Manc outside!"

"What can I get you lads?"

"Err, Three pints of Wards tha' knows!" I whisper in my best Sean Bean accent. As the poor aforementioned 'Manc' was led inside to have his wounds seen too. I heard him shouting

"I wouldn't mind but I'm a fucking City fan!"

We ended up in a club and Chris did what he did best, attract women left right and centre. Me and Daz were dancing like we were back in the Hacienda when Chris confided in me.

"I don't get it. I offered to buy her a drink but she says she just wants water because she's on an E?"

"Ok well that makes sense. What don't you understand?"

"Well when it's my sister's time of the month she can have a drink?" He may have been handsome but back then he was right naïve, was our Chris!

After a brilliant weekend we parted with Darren and caught the train home the next day. This time we hadn't borrowed his flat mates clothes and after shave but we did steal his cans for the journey home. Two thirds into the journey and I commented how all train announcers sound the same. I put on a Mark E Smith type voice and said

"Errr Ladies and Gentlemen, we are now approaching Stockport-ah! Stockport-Ah!"

Without a word of a lie, an unseen blind bloke and his dog got up and walked towards the doors. We didn't know where to look (neither did he actually). This was a fair way from the station and we couldn't tell him to sit back down because we were consoling our embarrassment with laughter that on all the trains in all the world, this one had presented us with such an awkward situation. A crazy end to a crazy weekend.

It's glory and honour the great man he said, there's nothing on earth like being a red.

32.   THERE SHE GOES

And so to the run in. I'd never been involved in a run in before, not really. Big Ron's teams had always faded away and ended up in 3rd or 4th. Fergie finished 2nd in 1988 but we were a long way behind. This time however, not just did we think we were going to win the league, we didn't care who knew.

'We're gonna win the league' is one of the greatest songs you can sing and we were singing it from the moment Robbo blasted home that volley on the opening day. So confident were we that we made sure we got seats in the Old Stand for the final league game of the season against Spurs, so we could be closer to the trophy presentation! In those days you were constantly on the phone to the ticket line (872-0199) to find out if the final game was going to be all ticket or not. Usually only the biggest games were all ticket and there was no real reason why this game would be except we were going to win the league! Of course the game was all ticket!

The confidence was of course partnered with nervousness. Everything was about trying to work out which game we would win it at and although Anfield was the preferred destination, Upton Park on the Wednesday before was very possible. Shay rang one day with some big news. There was a chance that the West Ham game would be shown Live on Granada if there was a chance we could win the league. When I asked him why he said he was checking the TV Listings for that night and at 8pm on ITV straight after Coronation Street it just said BIG FILM. His calculation was that if we could win the league then they would show it whereas if we couldn't then they would just show a Big Film like Jaws or something. They weren't saying the name of the film so as not to upset anybody if it got cancelled for Football.

"No Shay" I said to him, "it doesn't say 'BIG FILM' it says 'BIG. FILM', you know the film Big starring Tom Hanks? They jump on a giant piano?" This title run in was definitely doing strange things to us!

Before the big finish though came the small matter of The Rumbelows Cup Final vs Nottingham Forest. We had never won it in any of its guises and a day out at Wembley was always welcome. This year we were joined by royalty as both my Dad and my Uncle Danny came. That's right, my Uncle Danny who had never seen us win at Wembley. He made his own way from Chester whereas we had a different form of transportation. My Brother in Law Bertie is mad on airplanes. A proper plane spotter. One night over a pint of Joey Holts in The Roebuck, Urmston we hit upon the idea of Bertie dropping us early on at Wembley and then he would piss off to Heathrow for the day, happy as a pig in shit! After a hearty breakfast we hit the pub nice and early and it was great to have a few beers with my Dad and Brother as well as with Darren.

The game itself was nothing special. Brian McClair scored the games only goal and in fact I was more worried about Keith Curle winning the sprint competition before the match than I was about losing but thankfully, both the reds and John Williams, the flying postman, stepped up to the plate. For the first time in the club's history we had won a trophy for three seasons running but we had much bigger things in mind. We had of course won the Super Cup earlier in the season against a magnificent Red Star Belgrade team at Old Trafford. It was a single leg game due to the war in Yugoslavia and to this day I'm convinced that they went easy on us in some kind of pact so that they didn't have to go home to the bloody battles. Dejan Savicevic was incredible in midfield and tore us to pieces. It's no surprise he ended up at AC Milan. What is a surprise is that we had won that game!

With two trophies under our belt, all eyes were on the final ever First Division Championship as we knew it. First up was Southampton. This was our penultimate home game of the season and my very final game stood on The Stretford End. The new Premier League was coming and with it came all seater stadia. It was a very nervous Thursday night but the vital three points came from a Left Foot Swinger from Andrei Kanchelskis. I had stood on this terrace for 8 years hoping to win the league and it had never felt closer. We were 2 points clear with a game in hand. It was ours to lose.

We didn't have long to wait as just two days later we played Luton Town (A) whilst Leeds were playing at the same time at Anfield. As happened so often, both teams came away with draws. Our 1-1 courtesy of Lee Sharpe's goal was a definite two points dropped whilst Leeds might have been pleased with their point.

Just two days later again we were back in action again at home to Nottingham Forest, the team we had beaten at Wembley just a few days earlier. It's funny the things you remember. I was in The Toll Gate before the game and it was here that my Dad told me and Shay that he had diabetes and would have to make a lot of lifestyle changes as well as start injecting insulin. He was just short of his 50th Birthday, about the same age as I am now as I write.

Fergie decided to mix things up by dropping Mark Hughes and playing all three wingers in Sharpe, Giggs, and Kanchelskis. It seemed like a chance missed as Nigel Clough played centre half and looked like he had been there all his life. United were missing both Ince and Robson and were sadly lacking in midfield. Neil Webb played against his former club and had a stinker. With the game poised at 1-1 and United running out of time, Fergie swapped Webb out for Hughes and the former Forest man sealed his future career as a Postman by ambling off without a care in the world, much to the annoyance of the Old Trafford faithful who bayed for blood. As we pushed for a winner we left spaces at the back and Scott Gemmill broke away to give Forest all three points. It was an absolute kick in the teeth. Out of all the defeats we had that week, this was the game that afterwards I had cried. Leeds kicked off at Home to Coventry at 5pm knowing our result and the 2-0 win took them top of the table, 1 point clear having played a game more. The dream wasn't quite slipping away but the fat lady was putting her waders on!

33. LONDON CALLING

After two day gaps between the previous two matches it was once again two days later that we played against West Ham (A). This means we had played 4 games in 7 days. The FA had been asked for some help but it wasn't forthcoming.

So with the team playing on fumes, me, Chris and Darren got the coach down to 'The Smoke'. At least I had booked the following day off (because I thought we were going to win the league!) so I wouldn't have to be at work the following day. We wound our way through Canary Wharf, unaware of the massive building development that was about to change the landscape here but also unaware of how we would do. A win tonight meant we could technically win the league at Anfield on Sunday if the Leeds result went our way and that would change the landscape of our lives too. We were nervous and so were the players.

We were there in good times and decided to go in a pub called The Boleyn Arms which I'm sure you can imagine was full of cockney wide boys, hooligans and sex offenders. Definitely keeping our canisters down in here in case it got pwoper nawty! With a bit of luck we found a booth and drank our low quality Southern Beer and kept chit chat to a minimum. It was at this point that this bloke leant into the booth. He was enormous with his nose spread around his mush and a face like a balloon two weeks after Christmas. We shit ourselves and gasped wondering what he was going to say or if he was gonna just give us a striping. He fixed all three of us with a hypnotic stare and declared at the top of his voice in his best cockney accent

"I FOUGHT BRIAN LAHHHHNDON!"

"Err, nice one mate. Cheers" we mumbled hoping he wasn't going to demonstrate his pugilistic abilities that took on the former British Heavyweight Champion Brian London. It seems rather than come across the man who fought the man who fought the great Mohammed Ali, we had actually come across the local weirdo but it was still time for us to make an Irish exit.

Upton Park was in a vociferous mood. West Ham had already been relegated but in their final home game of the season they were determined to go out on a high and spoil our party. It's a shame Granada chose to show Tom Hanks because this was a night of high drama. Stood behind a very populated goal you could sense the apprehension in the air. The first half flew by with not much action but plenty of hefty tackles. 'A *War of Nutrition*' to quote the great Ellery Hanley. The turning point of the night and probably the season came in the space of 60 seconds.

United were pressing for the first goal and a hopeful cross saw Mark Hughes pull out a spectacular overhead kick. You could see it coming and were just waiting for the net to bulge only for Ludek Miklosko to pull off an incredible and improbable save. It wouldn't be the first time he would cost us the title. From the resulting corner West Ham broke away and Pallister cleared a hopeful cross, only for the ball to hit an unknowing Kenny Brown and ricochet past Peter Schmeichel. It was an absolute fluke and the kind of bad luck you just could not quantify or prepare for. As we shouted our frustrations, the local police openly laughed at the United fans and sang "We all love Leeds". This was happening right next to me and they were just waiting for one United fan to bite and they charged in batons waving to pull offenders out.

United huffed and puffed but to no avail. The final whistle saw scenes of jubilation from the Hammers fans who, let's not forget, had seen their team relegated. We shuffled in silence back to our coach to reflect that we were now 1 point behind with two games left to play and our next game was against Liverpool. The League title was no longer in our hands. I remember the coach had 5 Live on and John Virgo speaking to the presenter saying it should have been the greatest night of his life because he had just seen Jimmy White make a maximum 147 at The Crucible but he was distraught by the United result. So were we.

At least we had 4 days before our next match away at Anfield. Leeds were away at Sheffield United with a 12 noon kick off so we would know their result before we played. A win for Leeds would mean we had to beat Liverpool in a fixture that we hadn't even scored in since 1988. This time it wasn't Chris or Darren with me but my brother Shay. I had been to Anfield a few times but this was his first time and in fact the first League awayer I had actually been to with him.

Regular visitors to either Merseyside club would know that it's a perilous journey. If you go by train then you have to walk from Lime Street down Scotland Road and be on the lookout for the 'County Road Cutters' with their crude Stanley knives, often two held apart by matchsticks but having enough purchase that a striping off them would leave a wound so far apart, it could not be stitched.

We opted for the coach. No looking for pubs this time, just get there and get in. As we pulled out of the Old Trafford forecourt I saw all the arms from the coach in front of us go up at once. Sheffield United had scored! It was now 2-2 at Bramall Lane which was a more than satisfactory result for us if it stayed that way. Our coach driver found 5 Live and we listened intently as we made our way up the M62. Manchester and Liverpool were only 30 miles apart geographically but miles apart in every other way. Enemies from the days that the Manchester Ship Canal was built, taking trade away from Merseyside and into the heart of Trafford Park, the real birthplace of the Industrial Revolution. The Ship Canal used to actually go past the front of our house in Flixton. It was on the other side of the farmland right in front of us so the ships gave the impression they were gliding across the grass. Once a week the enormous 'Manchester Liner' would appear and we would race round to Irlam Locks to wave at the 'sailors'.

For over a century now the two northern giant cities had competed not just for trade, but in culture, music and of course Football. This visceral rivalry was normally demonstrated at 'The Rocket Roundbout' at the end of the M62 where Scousers would stone the United coaches from the overhead bridges. Today was no different and it was at this moment that it happened, 72 miles away in The Steel City. Leeds United scruffily cleared the ball away in the general direction of Cantona, summoned from the bench to try and capture the league title as he had the season before at Marseille. The Sheffield United captain and former Manchester City player Brian Gayle had the situation under control. However he rather miscued his clearance straight up into the bright blue sky, but it was ok, he could still head it back to his keeper, the future Manchester City player Simon Tracey. He hadn't accounted however for the keeper rushing out to collect the ball. Gayle's header looped desperately over Tracy and into the unguarded net to put Leeds United 3-2 and about to take a 4 point lead over Manchester United.

"FOR FUCKS SAKE" was the pretty much the words on everyone's lips on those coaches making their way towards Anfield, soon to be met by complete silence as the final whistle blew. For those final few minutes of the coach journey nobody spoke. Rather like a scene from the start of Saving Private Ryan, we made our way towards a destination that nobody wanted to go to and we knew was going to be hell. Nobody threw up though. Imagine someone doing that on the coach (eek!).

It got no better when we disembarked. We wore no colours but a scouser was straight into Shay's grill

"Eh lad, why don't you go to Wembley in a couple of weeks and see a real football team?" It was terrifying. Inside the ground the atmosphere was equally poisonous as The Kop sang,

"You'll never win the League". There it was, that song we had sung back in the days when the sun was warm and all seemed well with the world. Now we were in dark desperation.

We still had the game to play though. United brought back Robson and Ince, neither of which were fully fit and both of which hit the post. Liverpool scored early. Ian Rush had never scored against United in all his goal laden career. He chose today to do so. It was one of those days. Despite United's best efforts they had clearly run out of steam and a late breakaway saw Mark Walters make it 2-0 and finally extinguish our dream.

After the game it was a war zone. We narrowly missed being run over by the 'Bizzies' who were en route to one of the many fights kicking off all over the outside of Anfield. Rather like Saving Private Ryan not everybody made the journey back to Manchester. No one had actually been killed of course but there were only 11 people on the coach that returned. It was now 25 years since we had last won the league and maybe this was our last chance gone.

We sat in our Old Stand seats for the Spurs game the following Saturday but we didn't see the League Championship trophy presentation. That was happening at Elland Road. Things were about to change though, as we prepared to usher in a whole new ball game.

34. GIRLS AND BOYS

Football definitely took a back seat that summer. The European Championships took place in Sweden and we had little interest in Graham Taylor's moribund England whose only representation came from Neil Webb. Andrei Count-the-Shellsuits was playing for the 'CIS' or Russia in old money but he looked exhausted after that horrific end to the season.

I tried to put the football behind me with some good old fashioned drinking. Me and Darren had formulated a system where we did three quiz nights during the week and often won all three. The Fox and Hounds on a Monday, Yates's on Tuesday and The Victoria on Thursday. Sounds a bit like a Craig David song. I wasn't making love at weekend but it wasn't for the want of trying.

We did have a couple of jolly boys outings though, to Middlesbrough and Blackpool. Not hedonistic Ibiza I know but still, it was something different. Because my school was miles from where I lived and had a far reaching catchment area (one of the lads in my class lived in Chapel-en-le-Frith for fuck sake), I didn't have many school friends that lived near me in Urmston. There was one lad Dan who lived in Stretford who was the only one who ever got invited back to my house. Paul soon latched onto him and made us sit and awkwardly watch porn with him and teased my mate asking him didn't he want to go and have a wank? He eventually picked Dan up to demonstrate how strong he was and literally threw him across the room. Like I say, no one else came back to my house.

Darren however went to Urmston Grammar so his mates became my mates. They were all now in Sixth Form College together although one of them went to Middlesbrough Poly hence the trip up to Teeside. We squeezed into a car and it looked like it had given up the ghost at Hartshead Moor Services (scene of me and Barrie knocking over the Petit Pain on our way back from Leeds). This Service Station was cursed! We eventually made it though and we all took boxes of beer with us, the idea being to throw all the cans into a cold bath and then everyone could just get their drinks from there. Scott hadn't brought any cans with him though and said he would 'buy some when we get there'. He was a bit annoying and I could sense the other lads were used to this. Before the House Party though we went to the local to watch some Football and it was abundantly clear that he knew nothing about Football at all. He reminded me of the character John Thomson played on The Fast Show, the middle class Arsenal fan.

The party was in full swing and everyone was getting annoyed at Scott helping himself to cans from the bath without having contributed. 'Oh I just nipped out to the shop and got some whilst no one was looking'. Despite no shop being close by we had no choice but to believe him but this was one conniving muthafucker. Fast Forward to deadline day 2006 and West Ham United pull off the transfer coup of the decade by signing two sought after Argentinians, Javier Maschereno and, don't say his name out loud, Carlos Tevez and who was the man who put the deal together? Scott Duxbury. The very same Scott who knew nothing about Football with a Machiavellian streak! He is now to be found at Watford, firing Three Managers a season.

Thankfully Scott wasn't with us for the weekend in Blackpool. Andy was on the books at Blackpool FC and met up with one of his mates who had a drink with us. It was Trevor Sinclair. Seems to be a future West Ham theme going on. We stayed on a camp site, about 8 of us crammed into one big tent. One of the lads called Colin had invited a couple of his mates along but they pretty much kept themselves to themselves and had their own tent. They had left early and a pissed up Andy was giving them some stick whilst waving a bottle of beer about. They inexplicably called 999 saying there were a load of pissed up Mancs threatening them with bottles so it was no surprise when the police sirens we could hear got closer and closer. We huddled in the tent as first a police car came, then another, then up rolled the Riot Van! Then another! We were now shitting ourselves but in this moment of fear and potential arrest came two of the funniest lines I've ever heard.

Browny turned to us in the tent and said

"Let's pretend we are asleep". Oh yeah of course, they will take one look at us and say

"Oh shhh, they are asleep. Let's not disturb them!" We were all desperately trying to stifle the laughter when Darren said

"Imagine if they had Police Spiders?" That was it, we were hysterical. Sending in the Police Spiders certainly would have got us all out of that tent quickly! In fact any hostage scenario would quickly be resolved if they sent in the Police Spiders. On assessing the situation and having a word with us, the Police told the two lads that had called them to pack up their things and move on. They would stay on site until the two lads had left to make sure they had gone.

The new season was getting close though and me and Chris managed to fit in one pre season game before the new Premier League began. Having sat in the home end at Rangers two years before, this time I was standing in The Jungle at Parkhead (before its redevelopment). We actually missed the first 25 minutes of the game such was the clamour to get in and see the First Division Runners Up. It was certainly an eye opener. At one point we saw someone with a collection tin and a Dad shoving a fiver into his son's hand to put in the tin.

"What's that?" I asked

"It's for the Boys"

"The Boys?"

"The RA"

"The RA?" I had to question and he whispered in reply

"The I.R.A"

I don't think either me or Chris spoke through the Second Half for fear we might be mistaken for off duty British officers or something. Despite this we had such a good time we ended up staying an extra night and had to make up names on the train home as our return tickets were invalid!

Now we were ready for a life changing season, cue Richard Keys.

35. ALIVE AND KICKING

The 1992/93 new season certainly felt different and not just because the referees wore green. United had changed from Adidas to Umbro and it seemed like everybody had the new kits (I had the blue one). It was also the first year that I had my own self funded League Match Ticket Book (LMTB). I'd had an LMTB in the Family Stand for a couple of years but this was my first grown up one, sat next to Darren on the front row of K Stand (leaning on the Lin Pac Plastics sign). There was of course no more Stretford End and the ground both looked and sounded completely different without it.

Our first game was away to Sheffield United and despite the horrors of Anfield three months earlier, Shay had got the away bug and came with me and Chris. (I say got the bug, his next away game wasn't until Oldham in March). It was a boiling hot day and there was a fair bit of mither before the game as The Blades Business Crew put themselves about. Shay and Chris took one look at me in my brand new United shirt and moved away

"I'm not with him!".

We had only added Dion Dublin to our squad, a useful but unimaginative signing from Cambridge United. This was before he became better known for his massive cock and dislike of "Stairs going up to the bedrooms". We did set one record that day though. We conceded the first goal ever scored in the Premier League, Brian Deane the goal scorer in a 2-1 victory for Sheffield United.

On the coach home we were listening to Danny Baker on the radio and he was bemoaning the loss of Live Football on terrestrial television and how it was inaccessible to most who did not have Sky. He then said he decided to see what exactly

Sky Sports were showing on their one channel when the games kicked off at 3pm and he could not believe his eyes. Former professionals were sat watching the game on televisions and telling us what was happening! He was in stitches at this ridiculous format and there wasn't a cat in hell's chance of it catching on! Well he certainly got that one wrong.

We could not wait for the Wednesday though and our first game in our new LMTB seats. We lost 3-0 to Everton followed by a home draw with Ipswich Town. After our dismal collapse at the end of last season, things had got no better and we found ourselves bottom of the league. Our early form was awful and apart from a 2-0 win at home to Champions Leeds and, by all accounts, it was all pretty dire. Eric Cantona had played in that 2-0 defeat for Leeds and hit a spectacular overhead kick in the Second Half. I've heard a lot of Reds say they stood and applauded that piece of skill but I'm not having it. Straight after the game they probably went to The Lesser Free Trade Hall to see The Sex Pistols.

I had started seeing a girl around this time and took her to the Home game vs Torpedo Moscow, standing on the Scoreboard Paddock. A dreadful 0-0 game where the highlight was a two minute cameo by Gary Neville. A couple of days later I got the standard 'It's not you, it's me.' conversation but I know it wasn't me. It was Neil Webb, it was Danny Wallace, it was Russell Beardsmore. Don't say I don't know how to show a girl a good time.

The next day I travelled down to Spurs with Chris and Darren and threw myself into some serious drinking. We were in The Milford Tavern for a good couple of hours before kick off and genuinely, we ordered 9 bottles of Budweiser for the short walk to the stadium! Although we didn't quite get the last minute winners of the two previous seasons, we did get to see Ryan Giggs score one of the new Premier League's greatest goals with a piece of skill and finish that Barry Davies described as

"Brootiful". We sang the *"Running down the Wing"* song for the entirety of Half Time both in the stands and on the concourses. We know it was definitely sang in the Toilets as we had sank 9 bottles of Budweiser remember.

Although things had got off to a poor start, cue the official club video brought out at that time was called *'So Far So Good'* things were about to change for me both on and off the pitch.

I met a girl called Lisa and we hit it off straight away. First and foremost she was a Red! She had been to Wembley the year before for the Rumbelows Cup Final vs Forest and owned the same Blue Away Kit that I did (Twilight Zone Music) and we soon became inseparable. Unlike the previous Girlfriend who I took to Torpedo Moscow, Lisa came with me to two big glamour fixtures at OT vs Bury and vs Brighton and Hove Albion in the FA Cup! We also stood on The Kippax Corner for the Derby at Maine Road.

Late in November we went into Yates's in Urmston as we knew that my Mum and her Husband Barry would be there. As we walked in I saw a Blue I know and he started chanting

"Ooh Aah Cantona" at me. Alright knobhead we lost the league to Leeds last May, get over it. Then I saw my Mum who asked me

"Well what do you think?". I was totally lost and thought it was me who should be asking that question as Lisa was meeting them for the first time.

"Noooo, the Reds have signed a Striker. Foreign fella". My immediate thought was Darko Pancev from Inter Milan but then I remembered the Blue chanting at me…

"It can't be, can it? Eric Cantona?" "That's the fella" she said. The room span a bit and I did what most disbelieving fans did that day, I ran out of the pub to the nearest phone box to ring United Clubcall (0891 12 11 61). They confirmed the news and my second love affair of that month began.

36. POURQUAI ES TU DEVENUE SI RAISONNABLE?

Suddenly everything was coming together. Any worries about Cantona being booed for being ex-Leeds were quickly dispelled and he just seemed to be a United player. We suddenly looked like a different team. I went to Hillsborough on Boxing Day with Darren for one of the most extraordinary games of the season. I had lost on my last two visits and things didn't start well when we were 2-0 down very quickly. David Hirst, with whom the reds had been linked, was pulling onto the diminutive Paul Parker at the back stick and causing mayhem. We didn't panic though and Cantona started to dictate the play. Little flicks here, killer passes there, it was like watching a different team.

Chris Woods in the Sheffield Wednesday goal was having a worldie and for the first 60 minutes we were the better team bar the scoreline, then Wednesday scored a Third! Well surely that was that, the Turkey Butties were going to feel particularly flat this year but wait, the Reds kept pressing and Lee Sharpe was isolating the Wednesday Right Back, Roland Nilsson. Not once but twice Sharpie escaped his marker to set up Brian McClair who not once, twice scored past the previously impenetrable Woods. Now we were pressing for an equaliser. Sharpe got away again, Cantona was in space in the middle, the delivery was perfect, Cantona arrived right on time and missed it. A total fluff of a shot but the ball was still there, stuck in the Sheffield mud. Eric reacted quickest and stuck out a Gallic boot to prod the ball over the line. Bedlam! Eric ran to the United fans who had infiltrated the Lower Leppings Lane End (I was in the Upper) and The King had well and truly arrived!

Two weeks later Spurs came to a very wet Old Trafford and

Sharpe and Cantona combined again to give United the lead. The Stretford End was starting to take shape and some fans were in the lower section, cheering the goal in their club issued Rain Capes. In the Second Half, attacking the Scoreboard End I had the perfect view when everything clicked into place. Denis Irwin played the ball to Cantona who produced such an exquisite chip with backspin that you would deem it improbable on a golf course. The Irishman didn't even have to break stride to double United's lead and The Premier League had a moment that would be replayed over and over. The pass was immortalised in the film *'Looking for Eric'*, although an unpopular opinion I have is that, his pass to Solskjaer at Upton Park in late 96 was better. Soon 2-0 became 3-0 and even Paul Parker got in on the act and United were back on top of the league for the first time that season. Still no one dared sing 'that song' but Eric had been the reason Leeds had won the league the season before, could he do it again?

Unlike the previous season we weren't going to have any distractions in the cup. We lost to Villa (A) in the Coca Cola Cup and Sheffield United (A) in the FA Cup and I was at both of them! We jousted at the top with Aston Villa and Norwich City for whom Mark Robins was scoring aplenty after leaving United that Summer. Liverpool were going through a rough patch and we arrived at Anfield with our best chance in years of leaving with all 3 points. Chris and I went to scout out our seats and they were trash, towards the back of the Anfield Road Stand pretty similar to the seats I'd had the previous few seasons. Getting some refreshments before the game I bumped into an old mate of my Dads who was moaning that his seats were right on the front row and he preferred to be sat further back. Me and Chris both cast each other a quick glance which said the same thing

"Front row? Fuck Yeah!"

"Well I suppose you could swap seats with us if you like?" I shrugged and before you knew it we were right there, almost hugging Sparky as he gave us the lead. We won 2-1 and things were looking up. This was also the match we saw Ron Dixon from Brookside doing the Munich Airplane in the Main Stand.

That night me and Lisa went to Scott's 21st. Thankfully the caterers has turned up and we didn't have to drink cans from a bathtub. The win at Anfield had been massive, I was happily in a serious relationship for the first time in my life and I didn't see much of Paul anymore The first time he met Lisa, he told her she had a great arse and grabbed it. I did nothing despite wanting to. It was a guaranteed 3 points at Oldham Athletic on Wednesday Night to cement our place at the Top of the League.

We lost 1-0. All of the wobbles from the previous season suddenly looked like they would return. If we were finally going to break the now 26 year hoodoo and win the league, we were going to have to do it the hard way.

United actually sat in 3rd place when we went to Carrow Road in early April. A defeat here might just rule us out of the title race. Still with no Sky TV at home, we would watch those games at Urmston Sports Centre. It's funny how if I see clips of this game or the 3-1 win at QPR we watched there, I get the smell of chlorine straight away. There was certainly no ducking, no diving, no bombing or no err, petting for the reds that night as we carved Norwich open. First Giggs then Kanchelskis rounded the keeper Bryan Gunn to score before Paul Ince went round him and squared to the arriving Cantona to make it 3-0 within the first 20 minutes! The Sky commentary declared that Alex Ferguson was the calmest man in Carrow Road but there were certainly no calm men in Urmston Sports Centre as we ballooned away! There was to be more where that came from.

37. NO TIME FOR LOSERS

Due to financial difficulties and an unhealthy relationship with the Fruit Machines, Darren had to give up his LMTB in K Stand halfway through the season and sold it to Chris. Although I was disappointed not to be sharing the run in with one of my best mates, thankfully another was on standby. So it was Chris and not Darren who sat with me on that warm Easter Saturday Afternoon. I was feeling chipper as I got to spend the whole long weekend with Lisa who had to move away from Urmston, back to her parents in New Moston. We saw each other at weekends and tried to fit in at least one meeting during the week but a long distance relationship wasn't easy, especially with a League to win!

Sheffield Wednesday were the visitors that day, the Stretford End was almost finished and things were looking good. Wednesday frustrated us though and it was 0-0 at the break. Then one of those moments to bring on an ironic cheer; the Ref pulled a calf muscle! So there was a few minutes delay as the linesman got all his 'Ref shit' together and the Fourth Official became the linesman. The new referee didn't waste any time getting into the game and gave a penalty to Sheffield Wednesday as Paul Ince made an untimely lunge on Chris Waddle. John Sheridan stood over the ball. The Sheridan family were well known in South Manchester and one of his many Brothers (Mike I think) once got sent off in a junior game for kicking the fuck out of me during a game on Woodsend Fields. Now his sibling inflicted pain once again as he expertly rolled his penalty past Schmeichel and Old Trafford sat in stunned silence.

This time it wasn't to be Eric who dragged us back but a pair of Captains destined to get their hands on that new trophy. Bryan Robson came off the bench and soon got United moving again. Just like on Boxing Day, Chris Woods was magnificent in goal and it had all the feel of the Nottingham Forest defeat over Easter the season before. Due to the refereeing change and Wednesday's time wasting, we already knew that Aston Villa had been held at home by Coventry City so we couldn't let this opportunity slip. As 90 minutes ticked over we got yet another corner. Denis Irwin swung it in and Steve Bruce rose highest to send a looping header past the flailing Woods and strangely motionless Worthington on the post. We had got one back! Could we possibly get another?

Still the red tide marauded forward. It was before the days of the referee indicating how many minutes of stoppage time was to be played so nobody knew and we just kept playing. 96 minutes had passed when the ball ended up at the feet of Gary Pallister on the right wing, he looked up and sent in a pretty poor cross which deflected off the head of a Wednesday player and into the air. It was a time standing still moment as Steve Bruce attacked the ball and directed his header towards the corner of the goal. Back at the start of the Season when that end resembled a building site, that wouldn't have gone in. Even in January when they were dancing in the rain capes, it still wouldn't have been enough. Now The Stretford End was almost complete and the collective gasps of the crowd sucked the ball into the net and the Reds had won 2-1. There was that ballooning again! Not just me and Chris in the stands but Fergie and Brian Kidd on the touchline. It felt like this was the moment we were going to win the league but still no one sang that song. If we kept our nerve then the title would be ours.

Coventry City and Chelsea were dispatched before we were to face Crystal Palace at Selhurst Park. Just like the previous season we had made sure we had tickets for the final game of the season just in case we got presented with the trophy, so I had already bought tickets for the final day at Selhurst Park vs Wimbledon and had to sit this one out. Not to worry though as United had put big screens up at Old Trafford to watch the match. I always found this an odd experience, clapping corners whilst watching a big telly. Soon the word got round, Villa, who had kicked off 15 minutes earlier, were 2-0 down already at Ewood Park vs Blackburn. If we could get all three points we were within touching distance. It was a nervy affair which once again needed the calming influence of Robson from the bench. Halfway through the Second Half and with Villa now 3-0 down the ball came to Cantona on the left, he looked up to see Yellow and Green shirts in the middle and picked out Mark Hughes on the back post who fired home an unstoppable volley as only he could.

John Motson was providing the Live Commentary and had got a bit tongue tied during the goal commentary and as this was being edited on the hoof for that night's Sportsnight, during a quiet moment he suddenly shouted out HUGHES so it could be edited into the commentary. However back at Old Trafford watching the big screens the place went mad as they thought we had scored a Second. We didn't have long to wait though as in the 90th minute, with the Villa game finished, Cantona picked out Ince who drove home after a marauding run and that was it. We were 4 points clear with 2 games to go. We could win it next weekend vs Blackburn or even sooner if Oldham beat Villa. The sense of relief was palpable as finally everybody could sing

"AND NOW YOU'RE GONNA BELIEVE US, WE'RE GONNA WIN THE LEAGUE!"

38. WHAT THE WORLD IS WAITING FOR

So after the presumptions of the year before and trying to work out in which game we could win the league, this year we were no different. Do we want Oldham to beat Villa on the Sunday to crown us Champions or do we want to try and win it at home to Blackburn on the Monday? Of course we might just collapse like last year and lose both of our last matches, it was nerve racking. The fact that it was Bank Holiday weekend did mean we could party if Oldham did beat Villa. Latics were looking likely to be relegated and needed to win their last two matches.

I was in New Moston and considered going to watch the match in The Gardeners Arms but in the end decided I wasn't going to listen to the match and have a bath instead. I was in the Bath at my Girlfriends house when there was a knock at the door. "Latics are winning! Do you want me to bring a radio in?" So as 26 years of hurt and frustration finally came to an end, I was in the Bath! It was a wonderfully zen moment. Of course these days your phone would be pinging left, right and centre but in 1993, I just rang my Dad. He didn't answer and it went to the answerphone where his message screamed out

"Ooh Aah Cantona! Champi-ooooo-nees! Leave a message after the tone!"

Of course we had to go out that night so went into Oldham as we knew that a club there called Butterflies would be open. Yes it was as bad as it sounds and then some. As Fergie's heroes partied at Steve Bruce's house, we were at a club called Butterflies. The next day Lisa decided to come to the match with me. She didn't have a ticket of course but would watch it in a pub near the ground, she just wanted to sample the atmosphere and it was everything you would have hoped for. Town was rammed and there were flags everywhere. When I met my Dad and Shay at The Norweb club, my Dad was wearing a Champions T Shirt. I don't think I've ever seen him wearing Merch, before or since. At Old Trafford there was a massive flag from the Malta Reds on the front. Everybody wanted to be there that day.

The match itself was incidental. A hungover United winning 3-1. At the 80 minute mark a massive cheer went up as the trophy was moved into position. A year ago I could see the Football League Championship Trophy from my position at Anfield, it was in the ITV Sport box next to Elton Welsby. This time I could see the brand new Premiership trophy, glistening in the Manchester Evening. Finally it was time to get the trophy, bedecked as usual in Morson International caps. Steve Bruce and Bryan Robson lifted the trophy together and thousands of camera flashes captured the moment. We definitely felt like Champions now.

There was a rumour that there was going to be a party in 21 Piccadilly so Lisa and I went along. It was extraordinary. The place was packed with people in United kits. They ran out of Alcohol at about 1am. I saw Veg from Red Issue asleep leaning on one of the speakers, I may have taken my top off to dance and we never tired of singing *'We are the Champions'*. Keith Fane had made it over from his DJ duties at Old Trafford and announced that the team were on their way! We all waited patiently until finally, a pissed Russell Beardsmore was passed the mic and shouted "Yeah, we did it!" Hmmm.

I met Pete there and we hugged wildly. I think he had finally forgiven me for throwing up on the Rotterdam coach and leaving him stranded in the middle of the M6. We ended up in Albert Square and of course someone had a Football with them so we played, at 3 in the morning. This really was What the World was Waiting For.

There was still one match to go though. Wimbledon (A) at Selhurst Park. It was the biggest attendance in Wimbledon's history with over 30,000 Reds there. The night before was Lisa's Parents 30th Wedding Anniversary at Moston Labour Club. I may have overdone the Champagne as I slept right through my alarm. Lisa's Mum came in and asked me what time my coach was? I came round and suddenly realised it was in about 10 minutes and I jumped up stark bollock naked! Shay and Darren were booked on the Red Issue coach which was due to get into London a couple of hours before kick off so we could go to the pub. I clearly wasn't going to get that one but there were still the official club coaches. I rang and begged for a single seat and was in luck. Lisa's Dad drove me down and I made it by the skin of my teeth. It absolutely crawled through the London traffic and arrived at Selhurst Park with about 15 minutes to spare.

As I went through the turnstile, I wondered how Shay and Darren had got on in the pub when Shay appeared from out of the toilet and upon seeing me burst into song;

"Red Army!" Oh great, he's dieseled and I've got to sit next to him for the whole match stone cold sober (Darren had a standing ticket and had apparently been leading the singing in the pub with a lampshade on his head). Here's what you could have won!

United had announced that they would be bringing out the Premiership Trophy at the end of the match for all those Cockney Reds who hadn't been able to make it to OT for the Blackburn game. Legendary United songsmith Pete Boyle streaked naked across the Selhurst Park pitch. Obviously something he had always said he would do if he saw United win the league! I've got a lot of time for Boylie. Very funny, great taste in music and he had a small part in that day.

As the game approached 85 minutes and the Reds 2-1 up, people started to gather on the touch lines for a pitch invasion. Every time the ref blew his whistle, hundreds would spill onto the pitch and then have to be ushered off. After about the third pitch invasion, which included someone dressed in a full Mr Blobby outfit the referee had enough and blew the final whistle early. The players were mobbed and struggled to get off the pitch and it was announced that they wouldn't be doing a lap of honour after the match with the trophy after all.

As we walked back towards the coach park (different coaches of course) we saw the bloke dressed as Mr Blobby and some Cockney Reds weren't happy and challenged him.

"Oi you!"

"Blobby?"

"We never got to see the trophy because of you!"

"Blobby? Ah Blobby Blobby Blobby!" Mr Blobby never broke character and was soon windmilling into this bloke who had shoved him. It continued "Blobby Blobby Blobby! Blobby Blobby Blobby! Blobby Blobby Blobby!"

Someone then dived in and pulled the Cockney off the Cock of Crinkley Bottom and shouted

"Hey pal, you can't beat up Mr Blobby!"

The season had ended, we had won the league by 10 points and the European Cup beckoned.

39. WILDERNESS

And then it just stopped.
Not slowly reducing or missing a few games but completely stopped.

I was bowing out on a high after winning the league but from 1994-1996, one of the most successful periods in United's History (including two Doubles), I went to 8 United matches. In the previous 3 seasons I had been to 122 matches. The facts are that I had to do some growing up and some Adulting. Me and Lisa were still living 11 miles apart and it just wasn't feasible anymore. We decided that before any United Treble that I had to do a Treble of my own: buy a house, get married, have children, in that order. The first victim was going to have to be my LMTB.

We finally moved in towards the end of the 93-94 Season, buying Lisa's brother's house in New Moston. We moved on the day Eric scored 2 against City at OT. Of course one of the first things I made sure I had for the first time in my life was Sky TV so we set it up and watched The Derby eating chippy from Double Dragon on Hollinwood Avenue. This of course also meant that I moved to North Manchester having lived all my life in The Beautiful South. It would take a while to acclimatise and certain changes had to be made. A Barmcake would now be a Muffin for starters and the Launderette was known as The Bendix but other than that I was going to be ok. It was a much further commute to work in Old Trafford but I was also putting Paul further and further out of my life.

Remember that Ambulance that hit me back in 91? Well the compo' eventually came through so we got a weekend away in Paris. It was the first time I had ever been on a Plane, aged 22! We did all the touristy things and I was walking round Notre Dame wearing my France Euro 92 shirt with CANTONA 18 on the back.

I was approached by a bloke who looked at it like others looked at The Mona Lisa or Sacre Coeur.

"Erm, ou est buy, what's buy, erm purchase le chemise? En Paris?" He looked much relieved when I told him it was Allsports in Stretford Arndale!

Of course there were a couple of good games in those 8 that I did go to. The 9-0 vs Ipswich for starters. I also went to the 95 Semi Final vs Palace at Villa Park. I hadn't been to an awayer for 2 years so I was going to get mortal on this one. Darren and I caught the Red Issue coach and our 'bottle of orange' that was pretty much all vodka. I was definitely making up for lost time and missed away games as we kept the drinking going in The Dubliner pub near the Bus Station. Darren announced he was going for a Burger so I stayed put. 10 minutes passed, then 20. I had already drunk the two pints I had and didn't fancy the scrum at the bar. It was pretty clear that Daz had either just gone to the game (we had previous for leaving people behind in the Second City), been arrested or was dead. As it happened he had been arrested. He hopped over a fence and did a bit of dodging cars to get to the Burger Van which attracted the attention of the West Midlands Love and Peace Police. They said they could see he was a bit worse for wear and would he like a lift to the match?

"Oh yes that sounds great!" he said and climbed into the back of the van. After 10 minutes or so he said "I'm not getting a lift to the match am I?" He was right, he was taken to a Police Station in Walsall and chucked in the cells.

Once I had decided he wasn't coming back I went in search of a Taxi and found myself behind New Street Train Station. As a big fan of the Alan Clarke film *'The Firm'* I was a bit worried about Ovo and his crew coming to give me a striping but I did feel a bit vulnerable. As it was it was a bit of good old fashioned hooliganism that got Darren out of the nick. United and Palace fans had been fighting and a Palace fan had been killed by a coach (a big bus, not Brian Kidd). Back in Walsall, the Po Po hit the alarm button and emptied the station leaving Darren to find his way to Villa Park. He turned up halfway through Extra Time with United chasing an equaliser!

After the 2-2 draw we conspired to lose our coach, walk literally over the M6 on a bridge and then wave down a coach and buy our way back to Manchester. We decided against going to the replay on Wednesday!

Lisa and I completed the second part of our roadmap by getting married in September 96, the day of Nottingham Forest (H) and then honeymooned in Turkey where I managed to catch home games vs Rapid Vienna and Spurs in Bodrum. We toasted my new nephew Dean who was born whilst we were away and all was well with the world. But after the birth and wedding came a funeral (or hatches, matches and dispatches as we called it at the Evening News). My Uncle Danny was found dead in a field near his home in Chester. The Doctors thought he must have had a massive heart attack and was trying to get to a house on the other side of the field to call 999. We were all devastated but thankful that at least we had all got to see him at my wedding.

There was to be an addition to the family the following year when Hayley Lauren Taylor was born in North Manchester General Hospital. The love I felt for her was unconditional and couldn't wait to get her first little United kit. Unlike nowadays when the Parents can share 12 months of maternity/paternity leave, I was back at work the day after she was born. I caught the tram from work to see her in Hospital and it broke down just after Woodlands Road, the stop before my disembarkment at Crumpsall Station. I honestly felt like smashing the windows and climbing out to get to her or being passed down the tram like Crocodile Dundee such was the love I had for her. I often imagine there are steel girders that come out of my chest and keep me linked with all of my kids. Imprinting they call it in Native American Folklore (well I saw it on *Twilight* actually).

The North Stand had now been completed and after a year away in South Stand, my Dad and Shay now had Season Tickets in Tier 2. The view was brilliant but the 110 stairs were beginning to take their toll on my Dad and his knees and he started to offer me his ticket more and more plus I think he was finding it difficult to go to the games without his Brother next to him. I went to 7 games in 96-97 and then 11 games in 97-98 before he asked me if I wanted to buy his Season Ticket. Obviously it was a lot of money but we had found these things called Credit Cards so I finally had everything, wife, kid, Sky TV and Season Ticket. My first full season would be 1998-99. The big goalies coming up!

40. I WAITED PATIENTLY FOR THE LORD

The Season Tickets in North Stand Tier 2 were belters. Yes it was a bit of a climb and quite a high vantage point but you never had the problem of not being able to see the other end. Of course a good seat is only as good as the people sitting around you. I had someone in K Stand who hated McClair and called him fatty every week. Thankfully I had a good bunch around me. There was a guy who sat in front of us who looked like Vic Reeves. He sat with his Missus and held court every week. Liked the sound of his own voice. When we played Arsenal in 2002, the game that Arsenal won the double in, his Missus popped down to the loo after about 15 minutes and then someone came and sat in her seat at the end of the row.

"You can't sit there mate... Oh, alright Kev" It was Kevin Moran! Turns out that he didn't have a ticket and the turnstile operator let him in and said just to try his luck with empty seats! They chatted (loudly) about the 85 Cup Final and how we could have done with him this season instead of Laurent Blanc. Of course after a few minutes, Vic's Missus returns and coughs politely that he's sat in her seat.

"Oh sorry love, see you lads" and he was off to try and find another seat. Vic cast his Missus with a ferocious stare "You daft Cow, that was Kevin Moran!"

The season started with the visit of Leicester City and it took a last minute free kick from David Beckham to salvage a point. There would be a lot of that this season. As I was only going to Home games then the routine was pretty much the same every game. Get the Train from Moston Station to Victoria where I would get the Tram to Old Trafford Cricket Ground. Into The

Dog & Partridge for a few pints and a sing song and then stagger up the stairs! The exception to this was midweek games where I would go straight in the pub from work. Seems silly not to as I could see my seat in OT from my desk at work.

Fergie had boosted his squad with the arrival of Jaap Stam, Jesper Blomqvist and Dwight Yorke. It took Stam and Blomqvist a bit longer to adapt to the Premier League but Yorkie hit the ground running. He started up front with Ole Gunnar Solskjaer but soon was paired with Andy Cole and one of United's greatest partnerships was born. The feints, the step overs, the telepathic understanding, it was all there. They battled to be the first to score a Hat Trick at Leicester, Cole hit the bar to deny him but Yorke tapped it in to complete his treble, and also at Nottingham Forest where Ole upstaged them both by scoring four from the substitutes bench. Cole's goal in the Nou Camp has to be one of the great goals of that season, born from their appreciation of each other's position. Of course these were different times and they were a commentators dream 'The Soul Brothers' they called them. Big Ron was only one step from saying they had great natural rhythm. My friend was in Tier 3 for the FA Cup game against Liverpool. Now that's really high and after Dwight Yorke scrambled home the equaliser a cheer went around Tier 3

"Andy, Andy Cole!"

United got out of a Group of Death in the Champions League despite drawing four games. Although they shipped 11 goals past Brondby, the performances vs Barcelona and Bayern Munich gave real hope that this could finally be their year and they were to face Inter Milan in the Quarter Finals.

In the FA Cup they saw off a determined Middlesbrough who had beaten United at home a couple of weeks previously before being drawn at Home to Liverpool. Michael Owen scored very early for Liverpool and after that United tried everything for an equaliser. They hit the post, the bar and generally didn't have any luck at all. As the clock ticked over the 90 minute mark they were still 1-0 down. Beckham threw in a free kick and the ball broke loose to Yorke to score and send Three Quarters of Old Trafford into ecstasy and a few thousand singing for the wrong striker. Before anyone had the chance to check out the replay details in the programme, the ball was launched towards the Stretford End once again and the ball fell to the feet of the baby faced assassin to fire past David James. Incredible! From the depths of despair they had hit Liverpool with a blitzkrieg and finished their season there and then.

In the Fifth Round they faced Kevin Keegan's Fulham who were playing in the Third Tier at the time but with the backing of the Al Fayed family. Coming the week after the '9 goal thriller' vs Nottingham Forest. Nice one Big Ron; everybody expected a Valentine's Day Massacre but United won by a solitary Andy Cole goal. This was around the time of Top Reds not supporting England. The United lads were being booed by the Wembley crowds whilst representing their countries and it didn't go down well up in Manchester. In days gone by the Stretford End would sing

"Duxbury for England" for example because they wanted international recognition for our boy. In 1999 it was used as a mocking chant. If someone was having a crap game then it was pointed in their direction. A young Rio Ferdinand having a nightmare for West Ham and the crowd sing "Rio for England". Therefore with Keegan's Fulham losing and KK linked with the vacant England job then it's obvious what the Stretford End would sing

"Keegan for England" rang around the ground and Super Kev was visibly filling up. The daft bastard thought the fans were really singing for him and even cited it as the reason he took the England job! "When I heard those Man United fans singing Keegan for England then I knew the people wanted me." What a tool!

As we ticked into March then United were in the Quarter Final of both the Champions League and the FA Cup whilst battling it out at the top of the Premiership with Arsenal. People started to talk about the impossible Treble, never done before in English Football, but first Becks had a meeting with an old enemy.

41. ROD HULL IS ALIVE-WHY?

The visit of Inter Milan reminded me of the visit of Porto in the Quarter Final in 97. A vociferous atmosphere and right in their face from the off. Whether it be Jaap Stam not letting Zamarano pass or Giggs swaying and scything his way through countless European defences, these nights were special. All eyes were on David Beckham but weren't they always? The pop star girlfriend and the film star looks (I definitely would) made him a tabloid dream. It does however take away from what a bloody good player he was. The focus this night was on his rematch with Diego Simeone, the pantomime villain who was on the other end of Beckham's petulant flick that night in St Etienne and made sure the England man was sent off.

On this night in Manchester, apart from a sturdy handshake at the start, he didn't get near Beckham. His Machiavellian shenanigans will have to wait for another night in the future. Beckham put on a perfect display of laser equipped passing right onto the canister of Dwight Yorke who scored the games two only goals. For the return leg the 'Nerazzurri' were boosted by the return of a half fit Ronaldo. O Fenomeno was the best player in the world on his day but this wasn't that day. On that day his dive for a penalty may have resulted in a spot kick but not today. United rode their luck and it was no surprise when Ventola gave Inter the lead. The San Siro was like a bear pit at this point, baying for another goal and parity. But, rather like Montpellier back in 91 or The Superbock tinged second leg vs Porto in 97, this was one of those games where every United fan seemed to be at. They populated an entire end and the encouragement was non stop and it was at that end where substitute Paul Scholes scored the equaliser to send the United fans into ecstasy.

Another Dwight Yorke brace had seen to Chelsea in the Quarter

Final of the FA Cup so United found themselves in two Semi Finals with two very familiar foes. Arsenal in the FA Cup with whom they were also trying to wrestle back the Premiership title from and Juventus in the Champions League, whom they had played in the previous two seasons but lost 3 of the 4 games. Could United get revenge for the semi final defeat in 1984?

The first two games between this mighty triumvirate both finished level. Juve were the better team at OT and were disappointed not to come away with better than a 1-1 draw, especially as the equalising goal came in the final minute. In this season of late goals, that might just have been the most important. The FA Cup Semi Final was a poor 0-0 and they would have to do it all again on Wednesday night. Fergie rang the changes. Phil Neville, Butt, Blomqvist, Solskjaer and Sheringham came into the team. It was a gamble but the FA Cup was the least important of the three competitions left. United flew out of the blocks and got a trademark worldie from Beckham for 1-0. They should have got more but slowly and surely they were letting Arsenal back into the game. Then came a remarkable 5 minute period of play. First Bergkamp equalises with a deflected effort and two minutes later they think they have another as Anelka swoops on a Schmeichel error. Arsenal celebrate in the crowd but don't realise the game has restarted. As TV shows replays of the offside goal, Roy Keane hacks down Overmars and is sent off by David Ellary for the fourth time in his career.

Everybody has to regroup. United put everybody behind the ball and, although Arsenal smell blood, the flesh is weak. The game is limping towards extra time and hopefully, if United can hold out, penalties. That's until Ray Parlour has one last run at Philip Neville and he lazily attempts a tackle and brings The Romford Pele down. We have just gone into injury time and Arsenal have a penalty. The Treble dream appears to be in tatters. Surely Bergkamp will dispatch the spot kick, put Arsenal in the FA Cup Final and probably kick start their title defence. That's how it felt in that one moment. All three trophies suddenly seemed a mile away and Schmeichel wasn't the greatest penalty stopper in the world. The Non-Flying Dutchman looked nervous though and hit it to the keepers left but at a comfortable height and The Great Dane parried it away and then did that thing that goalies do and shouted at his defence. We were still in the FA Cup and 'The Treble' was still on.

Back home, in Moston, I was 'having kittens' as the phrase goes. I had a massive wee and opened the first of my emergency extra time cans of Boddies. This was tense and I prayed for penalties. As Vieira lazily gave the ball away to Giggs, I shouted something along the lines of

"C'mon Giggsy, give us one we can use on your highlight reel… highlight reel… highlight reel… HIGHLIGHT REEL!" It seemed a strange thing to be shouting but I just got louder and louder and as he weaved his way nearer and nearer to the Arsenal goal for possibly, given the circumstances, the greatest goal in the history of The FA Cup and possibly Manchester United and I'm just shouting

"Highlight Reel!"

The Incredible Dream was still on and now we had to plan.

42. LESSONS IN LOVE

Trigger warning This chapter does contain some racist language, the use of which the author does not condone..

As soon as we got out of our group we had one eye on the final. More to the point we had one eye on the Cathedral of Football that was Camp Nou, Barcelona. If United were going to be in the European Cup Final in 'The Nou Camp' as we called it, then I had to be there. Thankfully Shay felt exactly the same. Not going was not an option. It wasn't about 'The Treble', that was just an added bonus, it was all about winning the European Cup. We had heard about 1968 all our lives and it was time to make our own history.

Of course we had to qualify first and the 1-1 scoreline from the first leg certainly meant the odds were in Juve's favour. They had qualified for the last three finals so if anybody knew how to win a Champions League semi final, it was them. Therefore we agreed that if we did lose in Turin that we would go to the FA Cup Final vs Newcastle. A great occasion in itself but I desperately hoped I wouldn't be there.

A few of the lads from work were going to watch the game in town so I decided to join them. I normally would prefer to watch a big match at home but I could feel it in my water that tonight was going to be special. So it was several pints deep that we found ourselves in O'Shea's Irish Bar on Princess Street watching the big screens. I said a little prayer to St Patrick, reminding him that my 'Da was a Dub' and could the luck of the Irish be on our side? After 10 minutes the answer was a definitive no. United were 2 goals down in no time, Inzaghi with a deflected strike and bullying Gary Neville at the back post to put our European dreams very much on hold and I was mentally preparing to go to the FA Cup Final. However, it was merely a flesh wound as Roy Keane glanced home a header for a Captain's goal. We now had our away goal and another would put us in charge of the tie. That Irish luck was not going to stretch as far as our colossus from Cork as he overstretched trying to take a misplaced pass from Blomqvist and crunched into Zinedine Zidane. A regulation Yellow Card but one that would mean our inspirational skipper would miss the final. This was in the same stadium that 9 years previously the mercurial Paul Gascoigne befell a similar fate with a flash of yellow dashing his dreams of playing in a World Cup Final. Gazza burst into tears and was effectively a passenger for the rest of the game. Not for Roy Keane though, he rolled up his fucking sleeves and put in a magnificent and selfless performance to try and ensure his team still made the final.

Before halftime Dwight Yorke scored his 7th goal of the European campaign to make the score 2-2 on the night and now United led on away goals. If they could hold on for the Second Half then we would be there. After the first half goal fest it was much more cagey in the second half. Even though Juve needed to score, they appeared to have run out of steam and all their cunning and guile was no match for the blood, sweat and no tears from the magnificent Keane. There was another blow when Paul Scholes was booked and knew he too would miss the final. It was 9 years before he got the chance again. We had to park that up for now though. Juventus still looked scared of United on the break and we didn't know whether to stick or twist. Then came their moment. A massive goal kick from Schmeichel was mis-controlled and fell to Dwight Yorke. Some fancy footwork saw him one on one with the keeper Peruzzi. Time seemed to stand still. In those moments I saw everything flash before me. Getting my tickets, getting on the plane and being in The Nou Camp, Yorkie just had to go round the keeper and-PENALTY! It must be ref? Now who would take it, Irwin or Yorke? As all this went through my mind Andy Cole stroked it home and it was full speed ahead Barcelona! As I celebrated my glasses got knocked off and I was convinced they would be trodden on but that Irish Lady Luck had been smiling on me after all.

We bowled out of O'Shea's and headed for Piccadilly, stopping first at The Old Monkey, the Holt's drinker on Portland Street. I ordered a Pint of Holt's and an old fella sat at the end of the bar. He complimented me on my choice of pint and I told him I had been a Joey Holt's drinker for years, in The Nelson, The Roebuck and The Melville near me. Once again he gave me one of those 'mates for life' handshakes and drew me in closer

"Do you know what I like about this pub?"

"No, tell me"

"There's no N*gg*rs, P*k*s, W*gs or Ch*nks!" without asterix. It was one of those moments where it felt like the pub had gone quiet at that exact moment. Or that the people on the buses driving past all stopped and put their hands to their mouths.

"Erm, nice one pal yeah. Er guys, we're leaving! Leaving now!"

After such uncomfortable encounters, the topic of football brought the evening back on course and back on our lips; Away to the final, eh? We did a big huddle like drunk blokes do and vowed that we would all have a pint together on La Ramblas. One month later and I rang Mike from La Ramblas, the other lads were all still in O'Shea's and I was the only one who made it to Barcelona.

43. TOO MUCH TOO YOUNG

Of course we were still involved in a battle with Arsenal to get our title back. A post Turin hangover was possible but luckily our momentum kept us going. The 1-1 draw at Leeds could have been worse given our inexperienced centre back pairing of Wes Brown and David May. There were wins in the sunshine over Boro' and Aston Villa, draws with Liverpool and Blackburn. The dropped points at Anfield were particularly galling as it was a last minute equaliser from Paul Ince.

A Jimmy Floyd Hasselbaink winner for Leeds over Arsenal gave us the advantage on the final day. We were one point clear of Arsenal so a win would see us crowned Champions. Of the Four Premier League titles we had picked up under Fergie we had never won one at Old Trafford in front of our own fans. 10 days, 3 games, 3 trophies. This really was it. I got in The Dog and Partridge nice and early for some falling over juice and was chuffed to see Terry Hall of The Specials stood under the dartboard in the vault. I considered telling him my 'Too much Foo Yung' gag but thought better of it.

Fergie rotated again and brought in Sheringham for Cole. The ex-Spurs man hadn't exactly set the world on fire since his transfer the season before, but after a lengthy spell out through injury his return to the squad was a boost. Make no mistake, Spurs fans did not want to win this game and it was a very muted celebration when Les Ferdinand put the Londoners into a shock lead. United needed to wake up and before Half Time we did, a beauty scored by David Beckham. Teddy got the shepherd's crook at Half Time and the re-instated Cole scored within two minutes of coming on. A particularly sweet moment as many still remember his misses at Upton Park costing us the league in 95. The last 40 minutes seemed to take forever but there were joyous scenes as the ref blew the final whistle and we were champions again. Me and Shay hugged in our seats, man I may even have hugged Vic Reeves in front of us and although we were ecstatic to be champions it still only felt like Part 1 of something special. We had to keep something back for the two finals vs Newcastle United and FC Bayern München, Munich to you and me.

My Brother in Law took my ticket for Wembley. It seemed almost a blasé stroll in the park to win our third 'Double' in 6 years. Newcastle never stood a chance. Shay came round to watch it at my house but to be honest, all we talked about was the Champions League Final in a few days time. Of course whilst all this was going on we were trying to get our tickets for the final. I rang my Dad the day after the Juventus win but he sounded a little sheepish.

"Look there's no easy way to say this but I can't find the Bury and Nottingham Forest ticket stubs from the League Cup. I've looked everywhere but I think they have been thrown out". This was a very big problem. The token sheet had been replaced with the voucher sheet. Being a Season Ticket holder I didn't need to collect tokens anymore, just the ticket stubs from any cup games played. Namely Łódź, Barcelona, Brondby, Bayern Munich, Bury, Nottingham Forest, Middlesbrough, Liverpool, Fulham, Chelsea, Inter Milan and Juventus. Although I hadn't been to all the games, someone I knew had been and they had to give me the ticket stubs afterwards to stick on my sheet. My Dad had been to the two League Cup games and now we were two stubs down and this could very seriously affect our chances of getting a ticket for the final.

I was very distressed and thought to myself even though we didn't have the stubs, the Ticket Office must know that we actually bought a ticket? It must be on their records? So more in hope than expectation I made my way down to the Ticket Office on my lunch. I did have to laugh at the woman in front of me, she was very Cheshire set and approached the window.

"Yes I would like 2 tickets for the European Cup Final vs..." checks her notepad "Bayern Munich please?"

"Err, it doesn't work like that love" said the young lad behind the counter and he was still laughing as I approached him. Maybe his good mood helped me as I pleaded my case. He said it would have to be put before the Ticket Office Manager and I was to hand over my voucher sheet. Now I didn't have any vouchers at all in my possession and thought I had blown everything. A very nervous couple of days passed when a letter arrived clearly from United. I opened the envelope and took out the voucher sheet. Without unfolding it I could see the space on the sheet hadn't been filled with tickets and my heart sunk. As I opened it, in those two spaces was a signature. A name that strikes fear into followers of United away from home and a name that is so synonymous with bad news that it has spawned a new word in those circles... to miss out on a ticket application is to be 'chubbed' but on this day the name Arthur Chubb on my sheet was just 'Chef's kiss'.

We now had a full set of vouchers and had already booked our trip with Miss Ellie's, who were official partners with United. It had cost us over £300 for the day trip and the Season Tickets for the following season were due that week as well. I had spent over a grand on United before I had even set foot in Spain and now we were worried how much the tickets would actually be? We needn't have worried. £28 on one of the first two tiers and £12 on Tier 3. £12! Even then it wasn't a lot of money so we decided to treat ourselves to the £28 tickets. We still had to queue through the night though and as we pulled up at the United car park at 3am, my Brother was in his works Norweb van. The Car Park attendant asked

"Are you here for tickets lads?"

"No I'm here to read the fucking meter!" Shay was very stressed until the tickets were actually in our hands! A few hours later and our quest was complete. The dark days of Sexton, disappointment under Big Ron, laughing at the notion of challenging for the title in the early Fergie years, 5-1 vs City, collapse in 92, it was all forgotten in that moment because

"We were going to the Champions League Final!"

44. SOMETHING IS SQUEEZING MY SKULL

So before we head to Catalunya then I suppose the big question is why am I writing this book? They say write about what you know but *'Wanking into Bras'* would never make it past the publishers. I've made it clear that I don't deal well with confrontation and let's face it, there are going to be some questions after this. I suppose the simple answer is therapy. When my Cluster Headaches became so bad that I had to take voluntary redundancy from work, I fell into a spiral of depression and anxiety.

Depressed because I was mourning the person that I once was. The gregarious Taylo' who had sung with two bands and was always first up on the Karaoke, put on the best damn Quiz Night out there and sang

"Are we Hewden or are we for sale?" To the tune of *'Human'* by The Killers in front of the CEO and lived to tell the tale. There is no cure for Cluster Headaches so I could conceivably be looking at another 30 or 40 years of the worst pain known to man. Have a look on YouTube at an attack to get an idea of what we have to go through. Now I know that anyone reading this who has been through childbirth will be saying "Err, what's the worst pain sorry?" I know that childbirth is horrendous and I commend anyone who has been through it, be it natural, in a pool, pumped full of drugs or Caesarian. I have friends with Cluster Headaches who have given birth and they say that the pain is comparable but when you give birth, then you don't have to go through that pain again for at least a year as a minimum. With Cluster Headaches it is the same day again, the next day and the next with often no end in sight except the very end!

This is why they are known as Suicide Headaches as so many people just check out, not so much during an attack but just at the thought of a lifetime of Clusters. I made two very poor attempts to end it all. Trying to wedge my head between the sofa and the wall holding my breath and trying to drown myself in the kitchen sink. Pathetic as these may seem, my mantra was clear. I did not want to be alive and it was only the protective factor of my wife and children that stopped me jumping in front of the 81 to Derker. My marriage to Lisa had ended in 2005 and I started to see Loop in 2007 and knew on our first date that I would be with this woman for the rest of my life. Our second date was at her Mum's wedding for fuck sake, invited to sit at the top to table in a room where I knew the grand total of two people, Loop and her younger brother, Bear. Our marriage was in 2013 and was the greatest day of my life. I should have been looking forward to a long life with her when suddenly I had been struck down with this illness. It just seemed so unfair.

"Fear cuts deeper than swords" was a line used in Game of Thrones that I could empathise with. The fear of the next Cluster attack can be far worse than the Cluster itself. This is how my crippling anxiety began. I gave up drinking in March 2016 and haven't had a drop since. Partly because alcohol is a trigger for a cluster attack but additionally because I became scared of going to pubs.

I found myself under the care of the Rochdale Intervention Team mainly because of my suicidal thoughts and I began Cognitive Behavioural Therapy (CBT) in an attempt to at least coax me back out of the house that I had been stuck in for 6 months. After a few sessions to get a feel for therapy and my therapist I stopped him at the beginning of a session and said look there's something I need to tell you because it will help you understand the way I am, and told him the story of my abusive relationship with my Step Brother Paul. It was the first time I had this conversation with someone I wasn't close to; there are still close members of my family I have never told until now and there were a lot of tears. At the end Ross said he was so very sorry that I had been through that and he felt very privileged that I had chosen him to share it with. The next thing he asked me was did I want to press charges? God no, no I didn't. I certainly didn't want to get the police involved. Thoughts similar to many abuse victims asking questions such as

"Where is my proof?" and not wanting to further upset the metaphorical apple cart, "Maybe he has changed?", "What if its all in my head?" all of which I know the answer too. Were it be a friend in the same circumstance "What would I say to them in that position?" and eventually circling round to it all being my own fault. The roller coaster is real.

I did, however, feel a bit better after unburdening myself. I had always locked everything away in a box and tried to forget about what had happened but it was time for me to open the box and slowly let everything out. I began to remember things I had forgotten like the time we walked to Woodsend during our 6 week Summer Holidays to buy some chips for us and my Sister. Paul opened Marie's packet and pissed on them. Literally pissing on her chips. I knew this was so wrong but could not say anything for crippling fear of the repercussions it would place on me and anyone around me. It was literally a split second that he looked away and I swapped bags and I ate the chips that had been pissed on.

In Therapy they picked up on the fact that I liked to write and that had a one liner, or two, up my sleeve and it was suggested to me that because I use humour as a coping mechanism that I should write my life story or maybe even just write about United, Music, anything I was interested in. I certainly could have written about Music. As you have probably gleaned from the chapter titles, I am very much an Indie traditionalist. New Order, The Smiths, The Fall, The Wedding Present, The Stone Roses etc. This doesn't however mean that I'm a 'Well End' and have a Paul Weller haircut, wear Pretty Green and only listen to Manchester tunes. I've been to hundreds of gigs and there are plenty of stories to tell. These days I'm more into Female Electronica than Manchester Melancholia. I was encouraged by my wife to try and do something for me and I took tentative steps by joining the a Mind Anxiety and Support Group. We were like a mixture of *'Dear John'* and *'One Flew Over the Cuckoo's Nest'* to add fuel to the stereotype but I loved going there and it was a real wrench when I had to stop going because they had become a crutch, a comfort blanket but most of all good friends.

I also took great inspiration from a local author called John Ludden. I had read his magnificent book *'Once Upon a Time in Naples'* about the mercurial Diego Maradona and began to investigate his back catalogue. They were wonderful short stories about United, Boxing and growing up in this wonderful City of Manchester. I messaged him online and told him I was thinking of writing a book and he encouraged me and offered me any help should I need it. Hopefully he has made it this far and is reading it now.

I do feel I have a voice that needs to be heard. Whether it be back in the days of The TSAS in Red Issue or making people laugh on Social Media. My demographic on Twitter is very different and mainly filled with United fans but some of whom really make me laugh and vice versa and I reckon some of them as well as family and friends would like to hear my story… but the whole story, because I would be letting myself down if I put everything back into the box and packed it away for good.

45. ALCOHOLIDAY

Ten Days, Three Trophies. Two had been fought for, won and celebrated and finally we were on Day 10. It seemed that we had not just been waiting for this all week or all season, but all my life. My Dad went to the 1968 final vs Benfica with his Dad (Pop) and Brother-in-law. He loved telling the story about how they tried to find somewhere for a drink afterwards but the pubs were all closed. Eventually they found a Chinese Restaurant and ordered Six Bottles of Pale Ale.

"You must eat, you must eat!" said the owner.

"In that case..." said Pop, "we'll have some Prawn Crackers and Six Bottles of Pale Ale!"

My Dad had loads of stories like this. He tells one about the 1979 FA Cup Semi Final Replay at Goodison Park, which was won through a solitary Jimmy Greenhoff stooping header. After the game, my Dad was still buzzing so instead of driving home, he went to a pub by the docks and the Liverpool supporting 2-10 shift came in to watch the highlights on Sportsnight, not knowing the score. My Dad quietly asked for a pint to which the barmaid said

"You're a Manc aren't you?" My Dad's stunned expression and silence gave her the answer and she said "Don't worry, I'm an Evertonian. It's fucking great innit!"

Now me and Shay were ready to create stories and memories of our own. Having waved at each other across a foggy De Kuip Stadium in Rotterdam back in 1991, we were going to the European Cup Final together and there was no one I wanted to be sat next to more. Our flight was around 8am but was delayed by an hour. Manchester Airport called it the busiest day in their history so an hour isn't that bad. Our Miss Ellie's trip was on an airline called Air Transat which was Canadian! I think they just used every plane available and there was a bit of trepidation when the pre flight safety instructions were in French! Ah well, if we hurtle towards the sea I shall try to remember to shout

"Au Secours!".

Eventually we set off, hopefully not for Montreal, when we spotted a couple of familiar faces on our plane. Why if it wasn't actors Peter Howett, Joey Boswell from Bread, and Reece Dinsdale, Home to Roost, ID, and Coronation Street. I could only assume they were Reds and were just getting there as best as they can like the rest of us. There were a few shouts of "Shadwell Army" at Dinsdale and Shay dared me to approach 'Joey Boswell' and say

"Greetings!" Dinsdale did a Q&A on Twitter recently so I asked him if he went to the 1999 Champions League Final because I'm sure he was on my plane. He replied

"I had forgotten about that (imagine!) and yes I did go. I was sitting at home the night before when I got a call from Peter Howett who was a big Man U fan asking was I free the next day? 24 hours later I was sitting in The Bernabeu Stadium!" I unfollowed him there and then.

We arrived at Girona Airport about 50 miles outside the centre of Barcelona and were coached in towards the stadium. The driver dropped us near the Stadium and said he would pick us up from the same spot afterwards. This was the equivalent of an away coach parking up outside The Trafford pub and expecting to still be there at full time! We wet our whistle with a quick couple of Estrella's as we had a loose arrangement to meet up with Darren in Place de Catalunya and headed there. It was like a hyper Piccadilly Gardens with huge fountains and the El Corte Inglais Department Store towering over the Piazza like Debenhams over Burger King! We found a bar called Cafe Zurich and now the fun began. United seemed to outnumber Bayern Munich fans by about 10 to 1 and it was wonderful. The sun was shining, we were sitting outside a bar and singing United songs. This was my happy place. Shay had taken his camera and we got someone to take a picture of us (with our empties piled up behind us) and we both looked so happy. When I revisited Barcelona on Part 2 of my Honeymoon in 2013, we retraced our steps and recreated the picture with Loop standing in for Shay.

After a wander up La Ramblas and a couple more in a bar next to the Sex Museum, it was time to make our way to the ground. Now the nerves were kicking in! We were on a packed Metro platform when I felt a tap on my Shoulder. It was my Step Sister Heidi! We knew she was on holiday in Spain with her Boyfriend, and future Husband, Kieron. We knew this because they left their BMW at my Mum's house and Heidi's Dad, Barry, was ringing all the family and asking if we wanted to have a ride in the BMW with the roof down! Well it was a nice day so it would seem silly not to and we had a drive round, well Lisa did, I just waved at people from the passenger seat).

"What are you doing here?" I asked and Kieron replied

"I have friends in the Spanish FA so we came over from our holiday and we are sat in the VIP box. Where are you, behind the goal?" He answered rather smugly. A few seconds passed and I replied

"We've all been ragging your BMW around Urmston for the last week". That shut him up!

He's a lovely bloke really and we couldn't believe we bumped into each other. Heidi sadly passed away in 2003 at the criminally young age of 31. It was a massive shock which affected us all badly. My Daughter Hayley was 6 at the time and still sees Auntie Heidi as her guardian angel. In her honour we gave my youngest Daughter, Sunshine, the name Heidi as one of her middle names. So it brings me great comfort to know that somehow on that day of days, amongst all those thousands of people, that we found each other for those few brief minutes. I didn't know it at the time but there was no way we were going to lose.

46. SUCH A BEAUTIFUL HORIZON

There was more singing and nervous energy as we approached Camp Nou and a lot of that came from the United Youth Team who were all there in club blazers. I remember seeing a young John O' Shea pissed up and singing *'Keano's Fucking Magic!'* The Stadium is not actually that impressive from outside but that's more to do with the fact that it's dug into the ground. So the single concrete grey storey you could see from outside was actually the very top tier of the imposing stands behind the goal. Thankfully we had no problems getting through security and entered the bowels of the stadium. There was no fancy kiosk as such selling food and drink but trestle tables like at a Jumble sale. I got a drink and then something caught my eye. It was like the cliched long white tunnels you see in a film when someone is entering into heaven and in a way it was as this was the entrance up into the stands. I walked down the tunnel and The Nou Camp opened up before my eyes and I could see thousands and thousands of Bayern Munich supporters! All in denim jackets and sporting moustaches, just thousands of them as I was looking directly at their end. I then looked up and around me and realised that the rest of the Stadium was all United.

We were low down on the Second Tier and pretty much behind the goal. A perfect view for what was about to happen. Above us to our right were the United Youth team and if you look at any pictures of our end from that night, you can see a solid block of black jackets. That was them! Montserrat Caballe did a duet with Freddie Mercury on the big screen whilst riding around on a big milk float and the Bayern fans sang *'Everybody Get Up'* by 5ive. As kick off ticked closer you were hit with the realisation that every single pub you have ever been in probably has this game on their screen right now. Every fan of other teams you have ever met, even the angry taxi and dolmus drivers on your foreign holidays, are all settling down now to watch this match. You are at the epicentre of the footballing world... and we have no Keane or Scholes!

We suddenly looked very vulnerable without them. There were many different options available to Fergie. At Ewood Park a few weeks previously, he played Phil Neville in midfield. Ronnie Johnsen was also an option and Teddy Sheringham's Man of the Match display in the FA Cup Final meant he was in the running too. In the end he decided to move David Beckham into Centre Midfield next to Nicky Butt, Blomqvist on the left, Giggs on the Right. Not many predicted that. To win this Fergie was going to have to call upon that luck he talks about.

As with many of the big games this season, United started poorly. One down within 5 minutes to a Mario Basler free kick. It was a carbon copy of a free kick that Schmeichel conceded to Rivaldo in this stadium 6 months earlier. The rest of the first half passed without much incident. Our team had never started together in a first class match and it showed. Bayern had their goal and didn't really show much ambition for a 2nd.

Fergie made one of the great Half Time speeches, quoting Steve Archibald who lost the 1986 European Cup Final playing for Barcelona. At the end you have to walk past the trophy and you can't touch it. Don't let that happen to us. In the 2nd Half United huffed and puffed a bit but couldn't break through and as spaces started to appear then so did chances for the Germans. Mehmet Scholl and Carsten Jancker both hit the woodwork. It just looked like we were running out of steam. By now Sheringham and Solskjaer were on for Blomqvist and Cole and as time was running out we started to create chances. The German side were not going to try and add to their score and were running down the clock with substitutions.

With a couple of minutes to go, me and Shay gave each other 'the nod'. This non-verbal communication meant that as soon as the final whistle went, we were offskis. It was also conceding defeat, but there was always hope for one more chance. They say it's the hope that kills you but this is Manchester United and they never lost, they just ran out of time. The Third Official held up a board saying 3. Michael Jordan had his Last Dance, this was *'The Final Countdown'*.

When Teddy equalised it was an incredible feeling of relief, not just that we were still in the Champions League Final but because this whole adventure that we had dared to dream about wasn't going to end with a damp squib. We hugged wildly as our shins were battered on the seats in front of us, the bag I had hold of had nearly gone flying into the tier above us and Shay was now wearing a baseball cap that he wasn't wearing before.

When we finally came up for air we had another corner, we all know what happened next but, as I turned to my big Brother in disbelief, he wasn't there! I somehow knew to look down and he lay across the floor, having fainted when Solskjaer scored. I knelt to be at his level and for those few moments, despite the pandemonium going on around us, we felt like we were the only two people in The Nou Camp. Limbs were everywhere, flares were being set off and Big Pete was cartwheeling but we noticed none of that. Just a simple conversation as if we were back on Ascot Drive.

"Is that another goal?" He asked as he quickly came round.

"Yes, yes it is" I answered smiling.

"It can't be another goal?" he spluttered, tears and snot going everywhere.

"It is! It's 2-1!"

"Well get me up then you daft cunt!"

He wasn't the only one having trouble getting up as the Bayern

Munich defence were dotted about like victims in a car crash. Referee, Collina, tried to revive them but the race was run and the whistle blew. We had done it, The Champions League, The Treble, everything our collective hearts desired! I think I simply said nothing apart from

"I don't believe it!" for about 5 minutes and then I rang my Dad. I could hear very little but again shouted " I don't believe it!" and "I love you!" I just guessed he was on the other end. As a matter of fact my Dad did answer the phone and on hearing a high pitch screaming on the other end just assumed it was one of my sisters. When he realised it was actually me and I was ringing him from The Nou Camp it was too much for him and he handed the phone to my Step Mum,

"He's too choked up to speak."

The celebrations were incredible and David May achieved legendary status first by standing on a chair and then by making everybody quiet. You had to be there I guess… and I was.

47. BLACK MONK THEME PART 1

And what of the 20 years since. I am on my second Mrs Taylor, happily married to Loop and we have two amazing Children, Jimmy and Sunshine both born when I was in my 40's. Loop is also a brilliant Step Mum to Hayley who is approaching mid 20s now and all three of my children make me very proud every day.To get the chance to be a parent again was wonderful. When my marriage to Lisa ended in 2005, the financial strains that we were under was just too much. Once again my inability to deal with confrontation meant that I buried my head in the sand and hoped it would all go away. I couldn't simply hide in my room or go and stand outside Morrissey's house anymore. I should have done more to try and stop the rot but although I can see it now, I had no idea just how bad my mental health was at the time. I was terrified of opening the post and would switch the ringer off on the phone so we weren't bombarded by creditors all night.

I moved out of the marital home and into a Box Room at my Sister's house in Altrincham, something I will always be grateful for. The local shop selling 2 bottles of 'il Borgo' wine for a Fiver did a roaring trade. Of course the hardest thing about moving out was not being with my Daughter Hayley. She was my best mate and my separation from her tore me to pieces. It was a hell of a long way from Moston to Altrincham so I only saw her at weekends and had very little money left to do anything with her. My guilt at not being there for her as a full time Parent was crippling. I suffer terribly from Separation Anxiety now and if Jimmy and Sunny have to go anywhere like a sleepover then I'm inconsolable. I simply have to look at them sometimes and I'm in floods of tears. Therapy has helped me realise that this isn't just to do with them but a considerable amount of these reaction to my separation from Hayley. I simply never got over it and my brain can't cope with the 'What ifs' and unknowns and focus on the thought of the possibilities of it ever happening again with my other kids, even though I know that it never will.

My Dad tried to understand why me and Lisa split up and I said how there were a lot of things she had been party to that a lot of people didn't know about. He didn't understand what I meant and I said how she had to deal with the emotional baggage from me unburdening myself of all the bad things that had happened to me with Paul. He didn't mention it again but the following weekend we both took Hayley to the park which, of course, turned into taking all Pat's Grandchildren as well. Whilst they played he asked me what did I mean, what had happened with Paul? So I told him everything, absolutely everything. He took it all in and then said nothing.

A week or so later he rang me to say he had spoken to Pat and they believe that I'm exaggerating, I'm misremembering and just plain making it up and anyway did I know that Paul was bullied when he was little by Pat's ex-boyfriend. I couldn't believe what I was hearing and from that day I didn't speak to my Dad for 5 years. He had chosen to believe Pat and and not me or the level of trauma that had been inflicted by one of 'Her' children. In my eyes you don't ever stop loving your kids and wanting to protect them but it is a fundamental that you can dislike their actions and take responsibilities for your and their mistakes. I fully understand that she is going to side with her Son over her Step Son but I would expect the same courtesy from my Father. I just couldn't believe that they dismissed my trauma out of hand. I guess for some people that is just too hard to accept bad things did happen and that life in an Urmston sitting room, to parody Ivor Cutler, was so far away from what they thought and believed it was.

My Dad and Pat really were 'perfect together' and for many years she was the Mother figure in my life and for that I'm very grateful. However the truth is that he never got over the trauma of my Mum leaving him and will do anything and say anything not to unbalance the *status quo* and risk it happening again, even if it's at the behest of his own Children and Grandchildren. In fact he couldn't handle confrontation. Now who does that remind you of?

They sold the house in Urmston and moved to Penrhyn Bay/Rhos-on-Sea in June 2010 to enjoy retirement together. In August he was told he had Cancer and would not live to see Christmas. I had just had Disc Fusion and Compression Surgery and, against Doctors and Loop's orders, I made the journey to Wales that weekend. It was not the way that I wanted Loop to properly meet my Dad but I just had to make the best of what time he had left. The last time I saw him was in hospital the week before he died. His hair and beard were gone and he was very frail. I knew this would be the last time I would see him alive. He pulled me into him and said through tears

"If I let you down then I'm sorry. I'm truly sorry. There was nothing I could do about it!" and I knew that he was attempting to apologise for not believing me or at least having to give that impression. It broke my heart. I do regret not speaking to him for those years as it's time lost now. I do, however, still believe that I did the right thing. I had thought that the sub-plot in this book of tales would be between me and Paul when in fact, it was between myself and my Father.

He passed away in a hospice in Llandudno on March 1st. We got the call to try and get there on time but we never made it. We found out he had passed whilst on the M53 just as we were passing 'Face Mountain'. Straight away I knew that I wanted to do the eulogy and days later I stood before a packed out Altrincham Crematorium to read it out. Whether this book is well received or not, the eulogy will forever be the writing I am most proud of. Here it is in full.

48. BLUE SUEDE SHOES

"I'm here today to talk about a Father, Son, Husband, Uncle, Brother, Grandfather, Great Grandfather and Friend. James Mary Taylor was born in Dublin on May 8th 1942... or was he? For years he told us that he was born on the 8th but his official birthday was the 5th, or was he born on the 5th and the official birthday was the 8th? And was it because Gammie's writing made the 5 look like the 8 or because the registrar was drunk... we have heard both these stories and confusion still reigns today.

You never know with my Dad He once told me that the closing scene of *'White Heat'* starring Jimmy Cagney ("Top of the World Ma!") was filmed at Withington Hospital, he tried to convince me that The Bass Drum Pub in Stretford was the world's only revolving pub... except it moved so slowly that you couldn't actually see it move! And that the only way you knew it had moved was the view from the window when you left was different from the view from the window when you arrived. I suppose he was right about that bit.

Jim was the youngest of 5 children to James and Blanche AKA Gammie and Pop, with sisters Maureen and Blanche, and brothers Peter and Danny and soon after he was born they moved to Manchester. Jim went to English Martyrs Primary School in Urmston and then St Mary's School in Stretford. After leaving school he worked in the offices of Taylor Brothers, no relation, in Trafford Park before eventually finding employment at Norweb where he worked for over 30 years.

Jim married Pat Spencer in 1962 and the following year, James was born or as we all know him, Shay. Clare followed in 1964, then Marie in 1968, the second biggest event to happen in Manchester that year, and then in 1972 the youngest and most handsome member of the family was born.

The marriage came to an end, but in 1978 Jim met Pat Carnaby when both went to the single parent charity Gingerbread, years ahead of dating agencies or *'Take Me Out'* and the like and they were together from that moment onwards. In 1985, the two houses of Ascot Drive and Tanhouse Road were merged into a large house on Stretford Road and in 1986 Jim and Pat were married becoming Step Father in name to Jackie and Paul although he was already very much a Dad to them by then. He also took on the many many cats, Ginny, Tatty, Harry, Georgie, Jimmy, the one with three legs and of course their nemesis cat down the road… Grey Get. They lived in Urmston for 25 years before finally settling down in beautiful and picturesque Penrhyn Bay for what should have been a long and happy retirement.

In August last year Jim was diagnosed with Cancer of the Liver and the original prognosis was that he probably wouldn't make it to hear The Queen's Speech. Dad was determined however to make it to at least Spring, and to see his latest Great Grandchild born. It was therefore fitting that Dad finally lost his battle with this terrible disease on March 1st, not just seen by many as the start of spring, not just in St David's hospice in Llandudno that he loved so much on St David's Day, but the day after his Great Grandchild little baby Amy was born, who's picture he did see.

Grandad Jim had 15 Grandchildren in all: Michelle, Kerri, Rebecca, Jake, Joseph, Thomas, Luke, Shevaun, Mollie, Jack, Dean, Hayley, Charley, Franki and Mia and two Great GrandChildren in Lexi and Amy. He formed an amazing double act, with Bambar, as Grandparents.

Ah Bambar, I can't begin to think of the words to say to you today. The one thing I have to say is that you made my Dad very very happy. For all the sorrow and feeling of loss that we have, no one feels it stronger than you do and we will all do our best to help you through not just these trying times, but going forward to.

But let's remember Jim, the great gregarious figure who could hold an audience in the palm of his hands with his amazing stories. Who can forget the Father of the Bride speeches he made at Clare's, Marie's and especially Jackie's weddings where he told the story of how he went round to Jackie's to see if she needed anything but accidentally went in the wrong house, stood at the bottom of the stairs whistling the 20th Century Fox Music like he did, before being greeted by a big strange woman in a loose dressing gown with "Something winking at him!"

How he loved to tell the story about Shay seeing a monkey on the telly and proudly announcing "Look, it's Philip's brother!", Marie almost burning down Ascot Drive, Paul chatting away with Don King, Michael Nunn and other boxers after they went to the Benn vs Eubank rematch or Clare faithfully putting his tea in the oven as requested as he would be home late, not stopping to think that she had actually made him Salad. She still put it in the oven anyway!

Let's remember Dad singing '*Blue Suede Shoes*' in The Garrick and Red Lion, or the collection of part made up songs he had sang to the three generations of children… '*Silly Billy Silly Billy Five Pounds Ten*', '*Chin Chin Chinaman had a little shop*' or the haunting yet enchanting '*Has anybody seen my Poodle Dog?*'.

He didn't suffer fools gladly though and woe betide anybody who he thought did an injustice to him or one of his own, be it an Insurance Salesman, bossy bus driver or a neighbour with a blob of green jelly.

The other great love of his life was of course The Reds. He started going to Old Trafford in the 50s and used to run down to Davyhulme Golf Course to tell The Busby Babes the FA Cup Draw on a Monday lunchtime. His favourite player was, not surprisingly, Tommy Taylor and he was greatly saddened by the loss of his hero amongst others in the Munich Air Disaster of 1958.

Only a couple of weeks ago he insisted on being let home from Hospital to watch The Derby, although Pat says she knew something wasn't quite right when only she jumped up when Rooney scored his overhead kick!

I last saw my Dad 8 days before his tragic death. Although the hair and beard had gone, he was still gently singing songs to Hayley and regaling us with stories of how he had thought he had been visited by President Clinton and also how he thought he had upset a woman visiting her husband. He had overheard she was from Manchester and although he doesn't know why, because it wasn't like him, he shouted

"Are you a Bitter Blue!" Well this troubled him all night and the next day when he saw her again he beckoned her over and asked

"Excuse me love, do you support United or City?"

"United of course" she replied.

"Well I'm sorry if I offended you yesterday"

"Why would you have offended me yesterday?"

"When I sang 'Are you a Bitter Blue!' at you"

"I'm sorry sweetheart" she said "I don't know who you shouted that at, but it wasn't me!"

I realise as I grow older that I am turning into my Father more and more... if I have grown up to be half the man that he was, then I will be very happy. One last thing that he would want me to tell you all gathered here today, is that he never, EVER missed a penalty."

His funeral cortège was one of the last ones to stop on Sir Matt Busby Way outside the ground as the road was blocked off to Traffic a few weeks later at the end of the 2011 Season. My work colleagues at nearby Trafford House formed a guard of honour outside as we went past. It was one hell of a send off for a great and much missed Father.

49. BLACK MONK THEME PART 2

I'm sitting in my back garden now writing this final chapter and I'm wondering how many people will know its title comes from an album track by The Fall. There's that hurdy-gurdy music again my Dad was on about. The band I've seen the most is Half Man Half Biscuit at an impressive 47 times. I used to be on a Yahoo Groups Forum for them in the days before Facebook, Twitter etc. This was the original platform to form fan communities and I was definitely one of the main actors on that page. Yes the humour went over some peoples heads but it was an enjoyable forum.

One night, after Bayer Leverkusen knocked Liverpool out of the Champions League, I received a Message titled '4-2 to the Pharmacists'. It was a direct message from Nigel Blackwell himself, lead singer of the band and greatest living English Songwriter according to myself and many. It turns out he lurked on the site and he liked the cut of my j-i-b. He asked me to make myself known at the next gig and I could go backstage afterwards. I subsequently haven't paid for a gig since 2001. He does give me some weird and wonderful names on the Guest List though. Fun fact- he was voted the 57th greatest Merseysider of all time betwixt Rex Harrison and Andy McCluskey of OMD. From that day online I referred to him as NB57 and if you look on any Half Man Half Biscuit page online now he is referred to as the aforementioned NB57. That was my idea!

Why am I rabbiting on about Nigel Blackwell in the final chapter of my book? Well that's because it was on the HMHB Yahoo Groups Page that I met Loop. There was a group meet up at The Bankers Draft pub in Sheffield before a gig at The Boardwalk. A group of people meeting all referring to each other as their nicknames! I discovered that she was called Victoria, preferred

Tori or if you really got to know her you could call her Loop. She was also beautiful with 'come to bed eyes' and a right set of Bangers on her. This was 2004 though and I was still married to Lisa, whom was also in the pub at the time of meeting. She was with a couple of friends and was there for the first time seeing the band. With that good old question of getting to know new people, she asked

"So where are you two from?"

"Well we live in Manchester?" assuming she had no clue about Manchester as she had come with her friend from Hell, sorry, Hull and had fully adopted the East Ridings accent.

"Oh really, where about in Manchester?" she replied.

"Ah well it's a little place in North Manchester, you wont have heard of it!"

"Try me, go on!" The rest of the conversation between the four of us continued and it transpires that its one of those moments where having never actually met, she knew members of both Lisa's and my family, we had friends in common in real life, same dancing teachers as Hayley, albeit many years before, and to throw in for good measure, Lisa remembered Loop as a toddler in her pram as a young whippersnapper, as Loop's mother was the 'Brown Owl' and then 'Guide Leader' for Lisa's Brownie and Guide groups at Mills Hill. It's a small world but I wouldn't like to paint it!

After my marriage ended there were other gigs that we met at, Liverpool O2 Academy and Manchester Academy but I was never quite in the right place yet to do anything about it. We started chatting online and agreed to go for a date in Saddleworth where she lived. Let's just say I didn't need my return ticket back that night. We soon started dating seriously and most importantly she got on great with Hayley and vice versa. She wasn't just taking on a 35 year old bloke who has already been married but his 9 year old Daughter too. Loop was only 24 but luckily she was as smitten as I was and I got to say I was dating someone in her 20s!

She is a fantastic musician too, writes and arranges music, can play most instruments and, in her prime, was one of the best Brass Banders in the country. Nigel loved hearing all about this so he hatched a plan for Loop, my girlfriend, to play on stage with Half Man Half Biscuit. It was at Sheffield Boardwalk and the first of many times she played with them around the country. She even played Bass Guitar with them at Edinburgh Liquid Rooms in 2015. She is listed on the band's Wikipedia Page as "The Fifth Biscuit". As you can imagine, my wife is the coolest person in the whole wide world. Whether we are screaming our heads off because we are 10 yards away from Prince at one of his gigs or because we can't find the remote control or 'The Switch', as she calls it, she has well and truly saved my life. We moved in together into a suburb of Middleton, 2008, and were married in 2013. During my wedding speech I said

"We have had 6 incredible years so far, 4 Premierships, 2 League Cups, a Champions League and a World Club Championship!" We now have 2 beautiful children of our own in Jimmy and Sunshine plus I'm still incredibly close to my original 'big girl', Hayley, and although life is tough with our various ailments, I have never been happier. That's a strange thing to say for someone with depression but its true! As well as my Cluster Headaches and Pacemaker (in my heart, not a little athlete running 10 yards in front of me), Loop suffers from long term health problems and still manages to help me and the kids live a happy and safe life. We take everything day by day and hope for the best.

Like I wrote, times are tough but I still feel blessed. I no longer worry about the post or about Paul. What's gone on before still creeps up on me sometimes but I'm no longer worried going forward. I last saw him in 2013. I decided not to invite him to my wedding and he got in touch through Facebook wanting to know why? We agreed to meet in the Tesco Cafe at Old Trafford on my lunch break. After seeing him in a John Lennon T Shirt at my Dad's Funeral it suddenly hit me that I had nothing to be scared about with him any more. I considered asking a couple of the lads to tag along behind to make sure he didn't get handy but really I knew I had to do this by myself.

Without going into too much detail I finally got my man-jam together and confronted him. I told him he had treated me like shit all my childhood and I needed to be able to relax on my big day without worry of him kicking off (he also had previous of getting pissed at family occasions and causing mither). He took it all in and although I didn't think he would do anything in public (that's why I chose it!) my heart was beating out of my chest.

"Do you know what our Phil, I did treat you badly and I'm sorry about that. I hadn't really thought about it until you said just now but yeah, you're right I did. There was nothing bad in it and I didn't even know I was upsetting you. You should have said something you knob!" It wasn't the perfect *mea culpa* or Pope John Paul II apologising to Galileo but it would have to do. I had stood up to him for the first time in my life and it felt good. I also felt profoundly sorry for him in a strange way. I don't get to Old Trafford anymore. My current hit rate is about once every Seven Years. Just too many people there for my anxiety to deal with at the minute, it also doesn't help that we are fucking shit these days! I still watch all the games on the telly and Jimmy sits singing Viva Ronaldo and We hate Scousers! And finally, because we were trying for a Baby before Jimmy came along, we can pinpoint right down to the exact shag where he was conceived. I was wearing a kilt (that's for another time) and do you know what was playing on the radio that I didn't make it to the end of...

"Do do dooooo dooooo,

do do do do dooooooo!

Do do doooo do dooo,

'The Final Countdown'!"

Printed in Great Britain
by Amazon